WALT DISNEY WORLD WITH KIDS

The Unofficial Guide

Kim Wright Wiley

Prima Publishing
P.O. Box 1260
Rocklin, CA 95677
(916) 624-5718

To my children, Leigh and Jordan,
my two favorite ride-testers

Copy Editing by Eve Strock
Production by Rosaleen Bertolino, Bookman Productions
Typography by Janet Hansen, Alphatype
Interior design by Judith Levinson
Maps by Misty Parnell
Jacket design by The Dunlavey Studio
Author photo by Elaine Nichols

Prima Publishing
Rocklin, CA

Library of Congress Cataloging-in-Publication Data

Wiley, Kim Wright.
   Walt Disney World with kids / Kim Wright Wiley.
     p.   cm.
   Includes index.
   ISBN 1-55958-075-5 :
    1. Walt Disney World (Fla.)—Guide-books. 2. Family recreation—
Florida—Orlando Region—Guide-books.   I. Title.
GV1853.3.F62W349 1991
791'.06'875924—dc20   90-22203
                                              CIP

90 91 92 93 RRD 10 9 8 7 6 5 4 3 2 1
Printed in the United States of America

HOW TO ORDER:

Quantity discounts are available from the publisher, Prima Publishing, P.O. Box 1260, Rocklin, CA 95677; telephone (916) 624-5718. On your letterhead include information concerning the intended use of the books and the number of books you wish to purchase.

U.S. Bookstores and Libraries: Please submit all orders to St. Martin's Press, 175 Fifth Avenue, New York, NY 10010; telephone (212) 674-5151.

WALT DISNEY WORLD

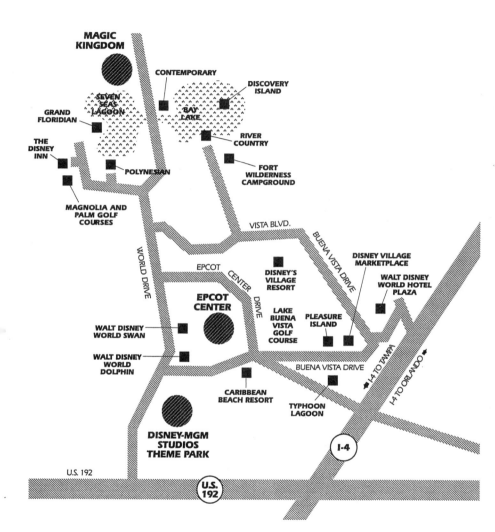

Contents

What Makes
This Guide Different?

Once upon a time, most people with kids didn't travel. Parents lucky enough to have supportive relatives or nannies took off and left the children behind. But more often people with children stayed home, figuring geographic paralysis was the price of parenthood. Tour buses all over the world are filled with people in their 60s who deferred their dreams of Maui or Moscow or even Miami until their kids were grown and out of the house.

Things have changed. No one is surprised anymore by the sight of an infant snoozing away in a four-star restaurant. A recent letter to *Travel and Leisure* magazine inquired about the difficulty of locating Pampers in Nepal. Today people take their kids everywhere, and they especially take them to Orlando, Florida.

Walt Disney World is the most frequently visited man-made tourist attraction on the planet. At first glance the place seems designed to cater specifically to families with young children. But it's not a small world after all, and actually circumnavigating the three major theme parks, the four minor ones, the nine hotels, and a shopping plaza requires as much organization and fortitude as undertaking a safari.

Guidebooks abound, but they rarely address the questions the parents of young children ask: Which restaurants are suitable for evening dining with a pooped

5-year-old? Where can we get a sitter? a Band-Aid? How much can you cut down on waiting in line by making reservations in advance? Will Epcot Center bore the kids? Is the extra cost of staying on the grounds of Walt Disney World worth it? Is it OK to take the kids out of school for the trip? Where can I breast-feed? Which men's restrooms have changing tables? Are Snow White's Adventures really that scary?

This guidebook takes into account the pace and pocketbook of a couple traveling with young kids. We feature those attractions, such as the breakfasts with Mickey and other Disney characters, that first-timers can easily miss but that can make all the difference to a star-struck toddler. Preplanning is essential—as you well know, a 2-hour wait up that's merely annoying to a lone business traveler can be downright disastrous to a single parent with hungry kids in tow. Nonetheless, some families try to wing it. You know the ones; you see them every morning, adults and youngsters standing flat-footed in the middle of Main Street, U.S.A., babies bouncing in the strollers, parents huddled over maps debating how to get to Dumbo, the Flying Elephant. This approach is akin to attempting to learn Lamaze after the contractions have begun.

To minimize problems and maximize fun, you must orient yourself before you arrive. If you follow this guide, you'll learn how to get tickets, maps, and reservations in advance and plot your family path. The book's list-style format makes it easy to consult, even on the run. The list format also lends itself to some repetition. For example, you'll find Pleasure Island listed under Minor Theme Parks, New Attractions, and Great Places to Go at Night. From October 1989 to May 1990, I passed out questionnaires and informally interviewed families leaving the rides. About 150 families responded to the written questions—their helpful comments and ratings and my tips are incorporated into the discussions throughout the book.

With just a little bit of forethought you'll be able to go against the crowds—moving clockwise while the thundering hordes are moving counterclockwise, touring Epcot while most people are in the Magic Kingdom, and, in the ultimate crowd-busting move, planning your trip during the off-seasons. If you manage to zig while everyone else zags, you can cut waits to a minimum and see twice as much as you would mindlessly drifting from queue to queue.

The basic rule when traveling with young children is to prepare without overplanning. You want to be familiar enough with the layout of the park that you can find a restroom fast, but not so driven by a timetable that you don't allow plenty of time for resting and savoring spontaneous pleasures. The first time my husband and I toured Epcot, before our children were born, we were moseying through the United Kingdom pavilion in the Epcot World Showcase Plaza. Street players had drawn a crowd and were directing volunteers in a hilariously funny mock-up of the play *Camelot*. My husband, Roy, was drafted to play Lancelot opposite a heavy pregnant lady from Minnesota; I sat on the curb snapping pictures and giggling. That event remains one of my happiest of all Disney World memories, and needless to say, it was totally unplanned. Fun stuff pops up all around the parks, but if you're grimly trying to make it from Fantasyland to Liberty Square on a schedule, you'll miss the key pleasures of this amazing attraction.

And pleasures are what this guide is all about. The three bugaboos of Disney World—the crowds, the heat exhaustior, and the expense—are especially tough on young families, and no amount of preparation will totally eliminate these problems. Walt Disney World is, after all, a 43-square-mile complex in the middle of

Florida, visited by as many as 100,000 people a day. It costs a family of four $102 just to get through the gate. You're going to get hot, be tired, and spend a lot of money—that's a given.

So why go at all? There's only one reason: It's the most fun place on earth!

What Makes Walt Disney World So Special?

The answer to this question is, in a word, detail. The entire Disney World fantasy is sustained through painstaking attention to detail.

True, the Disney World rides are tame enough that ki ls accustomed to the monster coasters at other theme parks may find even Space Mountain low-key. But if the attractions developed by the Disney "imagineers" don't rattle your molars or plunge you into water, they do rattle your expectations and plunge you into strange new worlds. In an attraction such as Pirates of the Caribbean, the atmospheric mischief begins in the queue, which winds you down into the bowels of a stucco fortress that grows danker and darker with every turn. The ride combines Audio-Animatronics, a catchy theme song, and an attention to detail so relentless that even the hair on the pirates' legs is real. You emerge 7 minutes later, blinking into the sunlight that spills through the market stalls of the Caribbean Plaza, fully understanding why Disney World insists its "rides" be referred to as "attractions." (The illusion holds up just as well at Epcot, where the Disney people have a bigger challenge: This time they're out to snooker adults into believing they're in Norway . . . or the land of the dinosaurs . . . or the human bloodstream.)

The theme parks were designed with the same precision that Disney animators brought to the classic Disney films. Walt was such a perfectionist that he never let four frames per second suffice if eight were possible. Now his successors are successful because of the same sumptuousness. Why not fly in monkey puzzle trees for the Japan pavilion? Hire George Lucas as creative consultant for the ride based on his *Star Wars* films? Buy the Muppets? Who says 11,000 dolls are too many for It's a Small World?

The authors of some guidebooks seem immune to the Disney magic, which is why they can describe Dumbo as a "sporadically loading ten unit cycle ride of the sort common to most midways" and advise you to pass it up. But it isn't a sporadically loading cycle ride at all, it's Dumbo, and no 4-year-old worth his salt is going to let you pass it up. The special charm of Disney World is that once we pass through those gates we are all 4 years old: impulsive, impatient, curious, easily duped, essentially cheerful, and ready to believe in magic.

1

★ ★ ★ ★ ★ ★ ★ ★ ★ ★ ★ ★ ★ ★ ★ ★ ★ ★

Before You Leave Home

ABBREVIATIONS AND TERMS
USED IN THE BOOK

WDW	Walt Disney World
MK	the Magic Kingdom
Epcot	Epcot Center
MGM	the Disney-MGM Studios Theme Park
TTC	Transportation and Ticket Center
the major parks	the Magic Kingdom, Epcot Center, and MGM
the minor parks	Typhoon Lagoon, River Country, Pleasure Island, and Discovery Island
on-site	the Disney-owned hotels that are on the WDW property, that is, the Contemporary Resort, the Polynesian Village Resort, the Grand Floridian Resort, The Disney Inn, the Disney Village Resort Villas, the Caribbean Beach Resort, Fort Wilderness Campground Resort, Walt Disney World Swan, and Walt Disney World Dolphin
off-site	hotels not located on WDW grounds
on-season	the busiest touring times; includes summer and the weeks surrounding major holidays
off-season	less busy times of the year, most notably spring and fall
the MK resorts	The Grand Floridian Resort, the Polynesian Village Resort, and the Contemporary Resort

the Epcot Center resorts

the Swan and the Dolphin (sometimes the Caribbean Resort is also referred to as "an Epcot resort")

WHAT TIME OF YEAR SHOULD WE VISIT?

1. September through mid-December is the best time of year for families with young children to visit. Crowds are light—about 25,000 visitors a day as compared to 60,000 in the summer months—and many area hotels offer discounted rates. Even the weather cooperates, with highs in the 80s and lows in the 60s.

There are disadvantages to a fall visit. You may not want to take your children out of school, and the theme parks do close earlier in the fall season. The MK often closes at 6 P.M.; MGM and Epcot remain open later. Because MK closes earlier in the fall, some of the special evening presentations, such as The Main Street Electrical Parade, are suspended during the off-season.

Fall is also hurricane season in Florida, so you run a risk of scheduling your trip for the exact week Hurricane Laluna pounds the coast. But Orlando is an hour inland, and even the worst coastal storms usually yield only rain. Furthermore, rainy days reach their peak during the summer months, not the fall, so in our opinion the advantages of autumn touring far outweigh the disadvantages.

2. If fall isn't possible, spring is nearly as nice. With the exceptions of the holiday weeks around Washington's Birthday, Spring Break, and Easter, springtime crowds average about 35,000—not as low as fall, but still far better than summer. And the weather is sublime, with highs in the 70s, lows in the 60s, and less rainfall in early spring than in any other season of the year.

In general, WDW runs longer park hours in spring than in fall, but schedules vary widely in the months between January and May. Call (305) 824-4321 before you leave home to check projected hours of operation.

3. If you must visit in summer, the first 2 weeks of June and the last 2 weeks of August are your best bet. Temperatures and attendance peak in July.

4. The absolute worst times, which people with young kids should avoid, are holidays. Christmas, New Year's, the Fourth of July, and other major holidays can pull in 150,000 visitors, which is six times as many people as you'll find on a typical day in October. Extended hours can't compensate for this onslaught of people, and although special holiday parades and shows are always planned, you're far better off at home watching them on the Disney channel.

5. Somewhat surprisingly, Fridays and Sundays are the least crowded days of the week. Mondays, Tuesdays, and Wednesdays draw the heaviest traffic.

HOW LONG SHOULD WE STAY?

1. It takes a family with young kids at least 4 days to tour the MK, Epcot, and MGM. In acknowledgement of this, the standard 3-day pass was eliminated in 1989 when MGM opened. Now 4- and 5-day passes, called World Passports, are offered and since the 5-day pass also admits holders to Pleasure Island, Typhoon Lagoon, Discovery Island, and River Country, it's the best buy.

2. If you plan to take in any of the minor theme parks, schedule 5 days; 5 days are also necessary for families who enjoy boating, tennis, swimming, or golf—or for those who'd like to tour at a more leisurely pace.

3. If you want to visit other area attractions, such as Sea World or Universal Studios, allow at least a week. You still should purchase the 5-day passport because it can be used on any 5 days, not necessarily consecutive ones.

SHOULD YOU TAKE THE KIDS OUT OF SCHOOL?

Even if you're sold on the advantages of fall and spring touring, you may be reluctant to take your children out of school for a week. Here are some ways to temper your guilt.

1. Rest assured that a single day at Epcot can be far more educational then a week of science and geography classes, and MGM is also surprisingly enlightening. Kids remember what they see. "That's a Viking ship," my 4-year-old casually observed while we were watching a movie one evening. "You know, like at Epcot." Another mother reports that her son was inspired to do an award-winning science fair project on drip irrigation after touring The Land pavilion.

2. Perhaps your child can work out a deal with her teachers beforehand whereby she'll do special reports or projects relating to subjects she'll encounter at Epcot and MGM. Here are several good suggestions:

- Into dinosaurs? Check out the Universe of Energy pavilion.
- Students of the natural sciences will find much of interest in The Land pavilion.
- Marine biology is the theme of The Living Seas.
- Missing health class? The Wonders of Life pavilion is devoted to that greatest of all machines, the

human body, and even has hands-on exhibits inside.

- Interested in geography? Some students have done reports on the cultures of countries represented in the World Showcase.
- Art students are bound to pick up pointers during the tour of the Animation Building at MGM.
- Drama students or even budding engineers will learn a lot "behind the scenes" at MGM's Backstage Studio Tour.

3. If your child is 10 to 15 and you think he or she might benefit from a more formal type of instruction, WDW offers three all-day seminars titled Wonders of Walt Disney World, which some schools accept for class credit.

At the day's beginning, students meet in a classroom and receive a book on the subject they'll be studying as well as a Kodak rental camera and free film. Then the group boards a special van with their instructor and begins a 6½-hour tour.

At the end of the day, participants receive a certificate of completion and a book with follow-up activities designed to help them expand the knowledge they gained during their tour. The three programs are Exploring Nature, Creative Arts, and Entertainment.

- *Exploring Nature*   During this tour, young people visit Discovery Island, Disney's 7,500-acre zoological park, study the ways animals and birds become endangered, and learn what they can do to protect their own environment. Students have use of binoculars.
- *Creative Arts*   Students get a first-hand look at the artistic process at work in WDW productions, examine the basic shapes in character art and animation, and receive their own sketchbook.

- *Entertainment*   Described as a "behind the scenes look at the hard work, dedication, and pixie dust it takes to put on a great show every time," the Entertainment program allows kids to meet Disney musicians, dancers, and singers. Students learn about lighting, props, and costumes while visiting a production and rehearsal studio.

General Info About the Wonders of Walt Disney World Program

1. Reservations are accepted at (407) 345-5860 and should be made weeks in advance, preferably at the same time you book your hotel room. Class size is limited to 14 students per session.

2. Brochures completely outlining the programs are available by writing

   WDW Seminar Productions
   P.O. Box 10,000
   Lake Buena Vista, FL 32830-1000

   If you want your child to apply for classroom credit for participating in the program, request an extra brochure for your school principal.

3. Cost for one seminar is $70.

4. Students are considered to be on a supervised field trip and won't need an admission ticket during the program.

5. Participants meet at the Wonders Greeting Area at the TTC.

6. Lunch is provided.

7. Not too incidentally, if your children participate in the Wonders program, mom and dad get a day free for adult pursuits.

Other Orlando attractions (most notably Sea World, which provides a guided tour on marine life) also offer educational programs. For details call

Sea World (407) 351-0021

Orlando Science Center (407) 896-7151

Orlando is only about 1 hour from Cape Canaveral, so if you have a budding astronaut in the family, it's an easy day trip.

IS IT WORTH THE EXPENSE TO STAY ON-SITE?

Staying at one of the Disney-owned hotels with monorail or shuttle access to the major parks is very convenient . . . and very expensive. Here are some questions to help you decide if the hours saved are worth the dollars spent.

1. *What time of year are you going, and how long are you staying?*

If you're going in summer or during a major holiday, you'll need every extra minute, so staying on-site is well worth the cost. (Another reason to book on-site in summer: In the Florida heat, it's nearly a medical necessity that you get young kids out of the sun in midafternoon. A nearby hotel room makes that easier.)

Likewise, if your visit will be for less than 3 days, you can't afford to waste much time commuting, so staying on-site is worth considering.

2. *How old are your children?*

If your kids are young enough to still take naps, staying on-site means you can return to your room after lunch for a snooze.

3. *Are you flying or driving?*

If you're flying, it may make more economic sense to stay on-site. The WDW transportation system is so efficient that you'll be able to manage without the cost of a rental car. But if you're driving to Orlando, consider an off-site location. You'll be able to drive into the parks at the hours that suit you without depending on those often-less-than-prompt hotel buses.

4. *How strapped are you for cash?*

If money isn't a major issue, stay on-site. If you're watching the budget carefully, stay off-site, or stay at Fort Wilderness Campground Resort or the Caribbean Beach Resort.

5. *How much do your kids eat?*

Food, in both the WDW parks and hotels, is expensive. If you're staying off-site, you can always eat at the numerous fast-food places along I-4 and International Drive. If you book a suite, fixing simple meals in your room is obviously cheaper, and teenagers can really load up at those buffet breakfasts the off-site hotels so frequently offer.

6. *Do you plan to see other attractions?*

If you'll be spending several days at Sea World, Cypress Gardens, or other big non-WDW attractions, stay off-site. There's no need to pay top dollar for proximity to WDW if you're headed for Busch Gardens.

7. *How far in advance are you planning your trip?*

Unless you're willing to book a room months in advance, forget staying on-site. Disney hotels fill up during peak seasons.

8. *Will there ever be times when your party will be splitting up?*

Does dad want to play golf in the afternoons? Do you have teenagers who'll be headed for Typhoon Lagoon on their own? Will there be times when it makes sense for mom to take the younger kids back to the hotel while dad stays in the park with the older ones? If so, stay on-site because the WDW transportation system enables you all to simply go your own way.

THINGS TO ASK WHEN BOOKING AN OFF-SITE HOTEL

1. Do you provide in-room babysitters? If so, what are their qualifications? How much is the cost? How far in advance should I reserve a sitter? Do you by chance have on-site child care? (Some of the larger hotels have their own version of a Kid's Club.)

2. Do you provide bus service to the MK, Epcot Center, and MGM? How often? How early—and how late—do the buses run? Is there any charge for the buses? Are the buses express, or do they stop and pick up riders at other hotels? *Note:* Take the hotels' commuting estimate and double it.

3. Do kids stay free? Up to what age? *Note:* This can be vitally important. On-site WDW hotels allow kids under 18 to lodge free with parents; the policy at off-site hotels varies.

4. Do you provide a free buffet breakfast?

5. What fast-food or family style restaurants are nearby?

6. Do you have any suites with kitchens? *Note:* No one's suggesting you should spend a vacation cooking. But many Orlando hotels have villa-style lodgings, and, obviously, if you can eat cereal and sandwiches in your room, you'll save significantly.

7. Do you provide airport pickup?

8. Is there a laundromat on the premises?

9. Can I buy tickets to area attractions through your Guest Services desk? Are the tickets discounted?

SHOULD YOU BUY A PACKAGE?

This question is a toughie. There are advantages to package trips, most notably that it is possible to save a good deal of money. It's also helpful to know up front what your vacation will cost. Often packages require hefty prepayments, which are painful at the time, but at least you don't return home in debt.

But package trips can also have drawbacks. As with buying a fully loaded car off a dealer's lot, you may find yourself paying for options you don't want and don't need. Packages are often padded with perks like a reduced greens fee, which are of interest to only a few families. Be doubly wary of the very cheap packages offered in Sunday papers. If a deal sounds too good to be true, it probably is.

More Common Types of Packages

World Passkey Packages

WDW itself offers a wide selection of packages, including the top-of-the-line World Passkey. Available only to guests staying on-site, the World Passkey is all-inclusive. Meals and tips, entry to all parks, lodging, transportation, and even such extras as rental of the popular Water Sprites and other sporting equipment are offered for one price. Visitors on the Passkey plan are issued a small gold card, not unlike a credit card, which they simply show whenever purchasing a meal, entering a park gate, or reserving a tennis court.

Such luxury doesn't come cheap. For guests at the pricier hotels such as the Grand Floridian Resort, Passkey rates run about $150 per person, per day. (Another drawback is that since all meals are included in the plan, you may find yourself gorging as a cruise ship mentality takes over: "We gotta eat it—it's free.") But for families who want to sample a wide variety of Epcot cuisine or who have kids who'd love to rent those $11-an-hour sailboats for a whole afternoon, the Passkey can offer not only total convenience but genuine savings. Call (407) W-DISNEY for details on World Passkey and other Disney packages and all on-site hotel reservations.

Delta Dream Vacations

If you're flying, check out the Delta Air Lines packages, which can include airfare, car rental, and lodging at substantial savings. Call Delta directly (1-800-221-1212) for brochures, or see your travel agent.

Travel Agents

Once upon a time, Disney paid no commission to travel agents for booking guests into Disney-owned hotels. Ergo, travel agents tried to talk clients out of staying on-site. With the opening of the Caribbean Beach Resort and the Swan and the Dolphin, however, WDW suddenly has a lot more rooms and occasional vacancies. Hence, policy has changed; Disney now pays agents commission, and agents are now much more likely to recommend packages that include on-site lodging.

Agents are also aware of other Orlando hotels that offer packages and are a good source of comparative rate shopping for families who want to stay off-site. Agents are your best source of information on the popular Premier Cruise Line, the "Official Cruise Line of Walt Disney World," which combines 3- or 4-day cruises to the Bahamas with WDW vacations. The ships leave from Port Canaveral, 1 hour east of Orlando, and the cruises are designed with families in mind. The Disney characters are even on board, and numerous child-oriented activities keep the kids happy, giving worn-out parents a chance to collapse on deck chairs.

Cheapie Deals

These are frequently advertised in the travel sections of major newspapers and offer extremely low rates. Proceed with caution, however. The hotels are sometimes as far as 30 miles away from the WDW gates. (With a rental car and an alarm clock, even this obstacle can be overcome, but know what you're up against.) Other pitfalls include tickets that can be used only at certain times of the year or extremely inflexible touring arrangements that require you to ride from attraction to attraction in slow-moving overloaded buses. A family trying to save money would be better off driving and camping, either at Fort Wilderness or in one of the other Orlando campgrounds, than signing up for one of these packages.

THE ULTIMATE COST-SAVING TIP: BECOME A DISNEY STOCKHOLDER

When you purchase Disney stock, even only a single share, you qualify for membership in the Magic Kingdom Club . . . and substantial discounts on rooms in Disney-owned hotels. Although the weeks in which the discounts apply vary somewhat from year to year, generally rooms are discounted 40% for stockholders from mid-September through mid-November and the first 2 weeks in December. Discounts of 20% are available from January 2 through mid-February and the last 2 weeks of August. These discounts coincide with the least crowded touring times of the year, so we find membership in the club doubly attractive for families with young children.

If you're planning to visit either WDW or Disneyland within the next year, you should purchase your stock as soon as possible because it takes about 8 weeks to receive club membership information and be assigned an identifying number. Only a certain block of rooms in each Disney hotel is set aside for stockholder discounts, and it goes quickly. (Some families reserve the same week year after year, and most stockholders are savvy to the fact that reservations should be made 6 months in advance.) When you call in to reserve your room by dialing (407) 824-2600, have both your Magic Kingdom Club membership number handy and second or third choices in mind for vacation dates and hotels you prefer. You may request the first week in October at the Grand Floridian Resort and wind up with the second week of October at the Polynesian Village Resort. But with price breaks like these, who can argue?

Disney stockholders receive other benefits:

- Discounts on theme park tickets.
- 10% discounts at Hilton hotels nationwide.
- Up to 23% discounts on National Car Rentals.
- 10% discounts on Premier Cruise Lines Disney–Bahama cruises.
- 10% discount on Delta air fares to Orlando.
- Reduced rates at certain WDW sporting facilities, most notably the golf courses.

- The Magic Kingdom Club also offers travel packages to other U.S. destinations, including packages to Disneyland.
- Stockholders receive quarterly reports, the most timely source of information on upcoming Disney attractions.

Obtain more information on the Magic Kingdom Club by writing

Magic Kingdom Club
P.O. Box 10160
Lake Buena Vista, FL 32830-0160
Or call (407) 824-2600.

ADVANCE RESERVATIONS AND TICKET PURCHASES: CALL NOW, AVOID LINES LATER

1. Get maps of the theme parks and general touring information by writing

WDW Information
P.O. Box 10040
Lake Buena Vista, FL 32830-0040

2. Purchase tickets to the theme parks by calling (407) 821-4321. MasterCard, Visa, and American Express are all accepted; the tickets will be mailed to you. If you'd prefer to pay by check, call first to confirm prices and then mail payment to

WDW Tickets
P.O. Box 10030
Lake Buena Vista, FL 32830-0030

Many area hotels, including all Disney hotels, let guests purchase theme park tickets through Guest Services. Inquire when you make reservations. (Guests of

Disney hotels get a small price break on tickets, which are waiting for you when you check in.) As of this writing, the following prices are in effect:

4-day passport (admitting holder to the three major theme parks):
Adult: $100 plus tax   Child (3–9): $80 plus tax

5-day passport (admitting holder to the three major theme parks as well as the four minor ones):
Adult: $125 plus tax   Child (3–9): $90 plus tax

1-day ticket (admitting holder to one park only):
Adult: $31 plus tax   (Child (3–9): $23 plus tax

Children under 3 are free.

3. Room reservations for on-site hotels should be made 3 to 4 months in advance. Dial (407) W-DISNEY for information on all Disney-owned hotels. The line is open 7 days a week from 8 A.M. to 10 P.M., and you'll have better luck getting through on evenings and weekends.

Room reservations for off-site hotels can usually be made later, perhaps a few weeks before you plan to arrive. Only the wildly optimistic should arrive in Orlando with no reservations at all.

Mistakes rarely occur, but it never hurts to call and confirm room reservations before you leave home.

4. Dinner show reservations, which also should be made from home, are accepted up to 30 days in advance for those staying off-site. Guests at Disney Hotels can make reservations upon the receipt of a room confirmation number. To reserve seats for the Top of the World at the Contemporary Resort, the Polynesian Revue or Mickey's Tropical Revue at the Polynesian Village Resort, or the extremely popular Hoop-Dee-Doo Musical Revue at Fort Wilderness Campground Resort, call (407) W-DISNEY.

5. Some of the breakfasts that feature Disney characters also accept reservations up to 30 days in advance; again, dial (407) W-DISNEY. Breakfast on the *Empress Lilly* riverboat at Pleasure Island, Minnie's Menehune breakfast at the Papeete Bay Verandah at the Polynesian Village Resort, or the "Chip and Dale's Country Morning Jamboree" at Fort Wilderness' Pioneer Park are best seen on the last day of your visit. The children will have had time to get used to the characters, who are large and a bit overwhelming at first; you won't be rushing to get to the theme parks; and the breakfasts are a nice send-off for the trip home. (Continuous-serving buffet character breakfasts are also available at the Contemporary and the Grand Floridian Resorts, but as of this writing they don't accept advance reservations.) The breakfasts cost about $10–$12 for an adult and $6–$9 for a child, with the Sunday brunches being more elaborate and more expensive. *Note:* During the winter off-season some character breakfasts are suspended—another reason to call ahead early.

6. If you're staying at one of the WDW hotels, Epcot dinner reservations can be made up to 2 days in advance by dialing (407) 828-4000. If you're not staying on-site, you'll need to make reservations on the day you plan to visit at the WorldKey Information Services under Spaceship Earth in Epcot.

7. Once you arrive, get up-to-the-minute information by watching channel 5 in WDW hotels or by listening to the Disney AM radio stations: 1030 in the MK and 810 at Epcot Center. And pick up daily guides to entertainment at the Guest Services stations of the theme parks as you enter.

8. No matter how carefully you prepare, WDW is capable of throwing you a loop by suddenly changing the theme park hours of operation. Call (407) 824-4321 the

day before you arrive for the next day's stated opening hour.

THINGS TO DISCUSS WITH YOUR KIDS BEFORE YOU LEAVE HOME

1. *Height requirements*   Get out your yardstick, because if your kids fall under the height required for riding Space Mountain (52 inches) or Big Thunder Mountain Railroad (40 inches), you should break it to them now. WDW vigilantly enforces these requirements, and there's nothing worse than waiting in line for an hour only to have little Nathan ejected unceremoniously just as you approach the ride.

2. *Layout of the parks*   Kids 7 or older should have some idea of the layout of the major parks. If you're letting preteens and teens roam about on their own, they definitely should be briefed on the location of major attractions.

Among the 150 families we surveyed (see our note about the survey on page ix, there was a direct correlation between the amount of advance research they had done and how much they enjoyed the trip. Visitors who showed up at WDW without any preparation had fun, but their comment sheets were sprinkled with "Next time I'll know . . ." and "If only we had. . . ."

The pleasures of being prepared extend to preschoolers. If you purchase a few WDW coloring books or Viewmaster reels to enjoy on the trip down to Orlando, even the youngest child will arrive able to identify the Swiss Family Treehouse and The Living Seas pavilion. A little knowledge prior to entering the gates helps you decide how to best spend your time and eliminates those "Whadda-we-do-now" debates.

3. *Classic stories of Disney*   If your children are younger than 7, another good pretrip purchase is a set of Disney paperbacks with accompanying audiotapes. Even though parental eyes may glaze over when "Dumbo" rewinds for its 3004th straight hearing, these tapes and books help pass the trip and familiarize kids with the characters and rides they'll be seeing once they arrive. (And if you find kiddie tapes too annoying, you can always bring along a Walkman for the children to use.) Some families rent Disney movies just before the trip as well.

4. *Souvenirs and money*   Will you save all souvenir purchases for the last day? Buy one small souvenir every day? Are the children expected to spend their own money, or will mom and dad spring for the T-shirts? Whatever you decide will depend on your pocketbooks and your particular interpretation of fiscal responsibility, but do set your rules before you're in the park—otherwise the selection of goodies will lure you into spending far more than you anticipated.

DON'T LEAVE HOME WITHOUT . . .

1. Comfortable shoes. This is no time to be breaking in new Reeboks.

2. Minimal clothing. Many hotels have laundromats, and you can always use Woolite to wash out underwear in your sink. Most families make the mistake of overpacking, not figuring in all the souvenirs they'll be bringing back. Disney T-shirts are not only great for touring but can serve as swimsuit cover-ups and pajamas.

3. A lightweight jacket, preferably one that's water-resistant.

4. Disposable diapers, film, blank VCR tapes, baby formula. All these are available within WDW, but at prime prices.

5. Sunscreen. Carry a tube with you and reapply it often. Sunburn is the number one complaint at the First Aid Clinic in the Magic Kingdom.

6. Juiceboxes are handy not only in the car for the trip down, but they're perfect to carry while you're touring because there are few places in the park where you can grab a Coke fast, and kids can become dehydrated rapidly.

7. A waist pouch (fanny pack) is a good alternative to a purse while touring, freeing your hands for boarding rides, pushing strollers, and holding onto your kid(s).

8. Sunglasses. The Florida sun is so blindingly bright that more than once I've reached into my purse for my sunglasses only to realize I already had them on. Kids too young to want to wear sunglasses need wide-billed caps to cut down on the glare.

9. Your credit cards—no joke. The Sun Bank, with numerous locations throughout WDW, gives cash advances on most major cards, which can be a lifesaver.

HELPFUL PHONE NUMBERS

All Orlando numbers have a (407) area code.

General information	824-4321
General accommodation information	824-8000 or W-DISNEY
Fort Wilderness Campground Resort	824-2900
Contemporary Resort	824-1000
Polynesian Village Resort	824-2000
Grand Floridian Resort	824-3000
Caribbean Beach Resort	824-3400
Walt Disney World Dolphin	934-4000
Walt Disney World Swan	934-3000
The Disney Inn	824-2200
Educational programs	345-5860
Tee times and golf lessons	824-2270
Tennis lessons (at the Contemporary Resort)	824-3578
Epcot Center restaurant reservations	824-4000
Dinner show and character breakfast reservations	934-7639 or W-DISNEY

2

★ ★ ★ ★ ★ ★ ★ ★ ★ ★ ★ ★ ★ ★ ★ ★ ★ ★

Choosing a Hotel

ON-SITE DISNEY HOTELS

Not content with merely dominating the entertainment market, the Walt Disney Company is now turning its attention to lodging the 10 million visitors who stream into Orlando each year. Orlando has more than 90,000 hotel rooms, more than any other city in the United States except New York, and an increasing percentage of these rooms are Disney-owned, that is, on-site.

Since 1984, WDW has added hotels at a record rate, with the architecture becoming ever more fantastic and fantastical. The recently opened Grand Floridian, Caribbean, and Swan resorts account for nearly 3,800 new rooms. The Yacht Club Resort, Beach Club Resort, and Walt Disney World Dolphin, all slated to open in 1991 and 1992, will provide another 2,700 rooms. The only real reason for WDW visitors to ever opt to stay off-site is price, but with the advent of the Caribbean Beach Resort—which at $80 a night costs scarcely more than a Days Inn—Disney is working to eliminate even that objection. The Port Orleans and Dixie Landings resorts opening on the WDW grounds in 1992 will add an additional 3,000 "budget" rooms to the tally, bringing the overall number of rooms on the WDW property to a staggering 19,000.

All this expansion means that even if a family decides to stay on-site, they still face a bewildering number of choices. Does the convenience of being on the monorail line justify the increase in price? Do we want to stay amid turn-of-the-century Victorian splendor, or is a fort more our style? Is it important to be near the swimming, golf courses, stables, and other sporting activities, or do we plan to spend most of our time in the parks? Do we need on-site babysitting?

Our surveys indicate that the Polynesian Village Resort is the favorite of families with young children, and

it enjoys a loyal repeat business, with some families reserving the same room year after year. Among more
budget-minded families, the Fort Wilderness Campground Resort and Caribbean Beach Resort also receive
high marks, but as in all of WDW, making the best
choice hinges on your awareness of what your particular family really needs.

The Magic Kingdom Resorts

Grand Floridian Beach Resort

Modeled after the famed Florida beach resorts of the
1800s and possibly the prettiest of all Disney hotels, the
Grand Floridian Resort has 900 rooms, with gabled
roofs, soaring ceilings, and broad white verandas.

Pluses
1. Convenient location on the monorail line.
2. A private beach on the Seven Seas Lagoon and
   numerous water sports.
3. Excellent dining choices.
4. On-site child care center.
5. On-site health club.
6. Exceptionally pretty rooms. The Grand Floridian
   is a favorite with honeymooners and others seek-
   ing a romantic ambiance.

Minuses
1. Pricey, with rooms about $225–$275 a night.
   Stockholder discounts don't apply, and even travel
   agents have trouble getting price breaks at this
   one.

2. Relatively new, with rooms sometimes difficult to book. Unless you're calling 4 months or more in advance, forget it.

3. The elegance puts off some families, who feel funny trooping past a grand piano in dripping bathing suits.

Overall Grade: B+   Expensive but luxurious.

Contemporary Resort
You'll either love or hate the Contemporary Resort, which has 1,050 rooms surrounding a mammoth high-tech lobby full of shops and restaurants. This place is always hopping.

Pluses
1. Located on the monorail line.
2. Fairly easy to book, and several discount packages are available.
3. Disney movies are shown nightly, and the Contemporary is also home to the Fiesta Fun Center, a giant arcade.
4. The standard water sports are available, along with tennis and a spa.
5. The Character Cafe is one of the best restaurants in the whole WDW for families, offering a chance to visit with the characters while enjoying an all-you-can-eat buffet dinner.

Minuses
1. It's loud, with a big city feel that's exactly what many families come to Florida to escape. "It's like sleeping in the middle of Space Mountain," wrote one mother.

2. Like the other hotels on the monorail line, the Contemporary is expensive. Expect to pay about $175–$225 a night, unless discounts apply.

Overall Grade: B   Convenient and lively, perhaps a little too lively.

Polynesian Village Resort

Designed to emulate an island village, the Polynesian is relaxed and casual. The main desk as well as most of the restaurants and shops are in the Great Ceremonial House, along with orchids, parrots, and fountains. Guests stay in one of the 863 rooms in the sprawling "long houses."

Pluses

1. The Polynesian offers the most options for transport. You're on the monorail line, but you're also within walking distance of the ferryboats. Launches leave from the docks regularly, as do buses from the Great Ceremonial House.

   Your best route to the MK depends on the location of your room. Near the lagoon? Take the launch. Near the Great Ceremonial House? The monorail is faster. On the beach? Walk to the ferryboat.

2. Private beach with an especially attractive pool and numerous water sports available. Like the beach at the Grand Floridian, the Polynesian has canvas shells that provide shade for napping babies and toddlers digging in the sand.

3. Minnie's Menehune breakfast, a popular buffet character breakfast, is on-site.

4. On-site day care is available; the Neverland Club is the only child care center that provides complete meals.

5. Numerous discounts apply in the off-season, including stockholder discounts.

6. The casual ambiance, with a series of small buildings spread out along the water, appeals to most families.

7. If someone in your party doesn't like heights, this is a better choice than either the Contemporary or the Grand Floridian because none of the longhouses are higher than three stories.

Minuses
Without a discount, expect to pay $175–$225 a night.

Overall Grade: A+   An outstanding resort.

Caribbean Beach Resort

This brand new, family priced, 2,112-room resort is located on 200 acres, with a private lake and white sand beaches. Each section of this mammoth hotel is painted a different tropical color and named after a different Caribbean island. More importantly, each section has its own shuttle bus stop, private beach, and pool. The Caribbean is so beautifully landscaped and maintained that it never seems like you're staying in a budget motel.

Pluses
1. Shuttle buses leave for major and minor theme parks every 15 minutes and run from 7 A.M. to 2 A.M.

2. The price is right, with rooms from $70–$95.

3. Parrot Cay, a man-made island with a playground, climbing fort, and small aviary, is especially fun for young kids.

4. Water sports abound, and the swimming pools here are very special.

5. This is one of the best places in all of WDW for renting a bike and exploring.

6. Cheap but tasty food is available in the fast-food plaza called Old Port Royale.

Minuses

1. The fast-food plaza is the only restaurant on the grounds and is always swamped with people. For more elaborate fare or faster fast food, you'll have to leave the hotel. The hotel planners should have put at least a burger and fries stand in each section.

2. Although the buses arrive regularly enough, they're nowhere near as swift as the monorails. Expect a slightly longer commuting time.

3. The place is huge. It may be a major hike from your hotel room to the food plaza or boat rental. If you have young kids, definitely bring your own stroller.

4. As of this writing, there's no on-site child care, which is surprising since the Caribbean was created for young families.

Overall Grade: A   Lots of bang for the buck here.

Disney Village Resort Villas

Designed for large families and golfers, the Village is a bit off the beaten track and offers a variety of one-, two-, and three-bedroom villas tucked behind the Disney Village Marketplace.

Pluses

1. Proximity to shopping and Pleasure Island.
2. Proximity to a major golf course.
3. The best on-site choice for large families.
4. Some of the villas are designed like treehouses, others have lofts and skylights.
5. Free daily housekeeping service.
6. Each villa has a kitchen complete with a coffeemaker and wet bar. Some villas have microwaves.
7. As well as golf facilities, you'll also find tennis, boating, and biking facilities and five swimming pools and a health club nearby.

Minuses

1. You're a long way from the theme parks, even by bus.
2. There is only one restaurant, although if you're cooking in your villa a lot, this may not be a problem. There are plenty of restaurants in the nearby WDW Village and on Pleasure Island.
3. It's very expensive for what you get, with villas ranging from $230 to $300 a night. (Grand Villas run as much as $850 a night.) Cheaper arrangements for big families can be made at the Pickett Suite Resort and numerous other Orlando hotels.

Overall Grade: C   Lots of space, but a heck of a commute.

Disney Inn

This quiet little place, located behind two huge golf courses, is often overlooked by the thundering masses.

Pluses

1. Shuttle buses run regularly to the major theme parks. You can also pick up the monorail at the nearby Polynesian Village Resort.

2. This resort is between the Magnolia and Palm golf courses, a great location if you've come to golf.

3. Tennis courts and a health club are also available on-site and are far, far less crowded than others in the WDW.

4. If you really want peace and quiet after a hard day of touring, here's the place.

Minuses

1. The Disney Inn draws a mostly adult crowd. There are very few child-oriented services such as playgrounds, child care centers, or character shows on-site.

2. There are relatively few dining choices on-site.

3. Prices run about $150–$175 a night, which is too high considering your limited transportation options.

4. There is no private beach, and consequently no access to water sports. You're allowed use of the beach at the Polynesian, but it's a hike.

Overall Grade: C   Come back sometime without the kids.

Fort Wilderness Campground Resort

A resort unto itself, Fort Wilderness offers campsites for tents and RVs as well as air conditioned trailers for rent. The wide-open spaces, perfect for volleyball, biking, and hiking, are a relief for families with children old enough to explore on their own.

Pluses

1. Fort Wilderness offers a huge variety of activities for kids, including hayrides, horseback riding, bike trails, and a petting zoo.

2. Proximity to River Country and Discovery Island.

3. Access to the MK via a private boat. Shuttle buses run to Epcot, MGM, and the minor theme parks.

4. Proximity to the Hoop-Dee-Doo Musical Revue, the most popular of the Disney dinner shows.

5. This is your least expensive on-site option, with hookups and tent sites as low as $35 a night. The trailers rent for about $150 a night but sleep 6 people and offer full kitchens.

6. Free daily maid service.

Minuses

Camping may not seem like a luxury vacation to you.

Overall Grade: A   If you like to camp, this is a great option.

The Epcot Center Hotels

The Walt Disney World Swan, Walt Disney World Dolphin

This huge convention/resort complex, the largest in the southeast, is connected to Epcot and MGM by boat service and bridges. When Disney's Yacht and Beach Club Resort opens in early 1991, the three hotels will share Fantasy Lagoon, a full-scale water resort with boating, snorkeling, and corkscrew slides. Also coming in 1991 is a boardwalk complex that will feature a midway, thrill rides, and live entertainment.

Pluses

1. Disney is aggressively going after the convention trade with the Swan. If a working parent is lucky, she can score a free family vacation here.

2. Transportation to Epcot and MGM by water taxi or shuttle bus, with a slightly longer shuttle ride to the MK. These hotels offer extremely easy access to Epcot, with a private entrance into the back of the World Showcase. Dolphin and Swan guests headed for Epcot can completely avoid arriving and departing crowds. (You even have your own stroller rental booth, in the France pavilion, and breakfast at the Boulangerie Patisserie is sublime.)

3. Camp Swan offers on-site child care from 4 P.M. to midnight.

Minuses

1. Expensive, at $200–$265 a night.

2. Because of the proximity to Epcot and MGM and the fact the Swan is gunning for the convention trade, this is an adult-oriented resort, with a citified atmosphere. If your kids are young and rambunctious, go elsewhere.

3. At present (although construction is still underway), the Swan and Dolphin share a small beach. The pools are tiny and cramped.

Overall Grade: B   A great place to go if the company is picking up the tab. Otherwise, try the Grand Floridian or the Polynesian first.

GENERAL INFORMATION
ON THE WDW HOTELS

1. A deposit equal to one night's lodging is required within 21 days after you make your reservation. You may pay by check or with a MasterCard or a Visa or American Express card.

2. Refund of your full deposit will be made if your reservation is canceled at least 48 hours prior to arrival.

3. All Disney hotels operate under the family plan, meaning that kids 18 and under stay free with parents.

4. Check in time is 3 P.M. at most resorts but 4 P.M. at the Village Resort and 1 P.M. at Fort Wilderness. You can pick up your tickets in the morning at Guest Services, however, and tour until midafternoon. Return to your hotel then and check in.

5. Check out time is 11 A.M., but you needn't lose a day of touring. Check out early in the morning and either store your bags with the concierge or take them to your car and then go enjoy your last day in the parks.

6. You'll be issued a resort ID when you check in, which allows you to charge meals, drinks, and souvenirs to your room as well as giving you access to all WDW transportation.

7. If you can't manage to get booked on-site, many of the same policies and amenities apply to the seven hotels in the Disney Village Hotel Plaza.

8. "Value Season" usually runs in January, May, and from mid-August to mid-December. Any guests booking rooms during this time, even those who

don't qualify for stockholder discounts or who aren't buying a package, will receive a slightly reduced rate. /

OFF-SITE HOTELS: GREAT PLACES FOR FAMILIES

1. *Hilton at Disney Village Hotel Plaza*
Conveniently located with shuttle service to nearly all area attractions, the Hilton has the additional boon of a Youth Hotel for kids 3–12, open from 5 P.M. until midnight, with a charge of $4 an hour. The hotel has a playroom, large-screen TV, Nintendo games, and even a six-bed dormitory complete with teddy bears so sleepy preschoolers can be bedded down. Youth Hotel services aren't limited to Hilton guests, and if parents are dining in the spiffy American Vineyards restaurant in the Hilton lobby, 3 hours of child care is complimentary—the counselors will accompany the kids to a burger-and-shakes meal at the soda shop next door.
    Rates are $140–$180. Call 1-800-445-8667 or (407) 827-4000.

2. *Stouffer Orlando Resort*
Huge and gorgeous, with a 10-story atrium so cavernous that indoor fireworks displays are set at New Year's and the Fourth of July, the Stouffer is the only area hotel to offer drop-off sitting for babies and toddlers. Infants as young as 6 weeks are welcome at "Shamu's Playhouse," named for the Sea World star who lives just across the street. The Playhouse offers a staff of trained counselors, an all-sand playground, and a private wading pool. Open from 8 A.M. to 11 P.M. at a cost of $4.50 an hour (50¢ an hour more for each additional child), this is surely the child care bargain in Orlando. It is also the

only on-site center open in the morning for parents who'd like to sneak in a game of tennis or golf.

Diners at Haifeng or Atlantis, the flagship restaurants of the Stouffer, receive three complimentary hours of child care, as do diners at the Sunday brunch. At the brunch, 400 feet of food line the atrium, offering everything from strawberry soup to sushi to Rock Cornish game hens for $19.95. Kids chow down at a separate brunch ($8.95) starring Peaches the Clown and a spread geared to younger tastes.

Rates are $120–$180. Call (407) 351-5555 or 1-800-327-6677.

3. *Pickett Suite at Disney Village Hotel Plaza*

The Pickett is the best choice for large families because every room is a suite, with a living room, wet bar, coffeemaker, microwave, and—most invaluable to families with preteens—a refrigerator well stocked with snacks and free juices. The kitchens allow you to cook some meals on-site, a definite savings in a town where Cokes can go for $2 a pop. Perhaps for this reason the Pickett draws almost exclusively a family crowd. The biggest bonus is a free buffet breakfast so huge you can coast on those carbohydrates until midafternoon.

Rates are $120–$170. Call 1-800-742-5388 or (407) 934-1000.

4. *Sonesta Village*

If you'd like a place a bit off the beaten path, try Sonesta Village, a virtual hamlet of townhomes surrounding a 300-acre lake. Sand Lake offers parasailing, jet skiing, windsurfing, and a panorama of other water sports, including my personal favorite, Lying on the Beach Watching the Snowy Egrets. The townhomes, like the Pickett Suite, have kitchens so you can fix a cheap batch of spaghetti.

The Sonesta has an elaborate Kid's Club with T-shirts to prove it. Trained counselors lead children 4–12 through volleyball, crafts, sack races, and other camplike events. Amazingly, the club is free to all guests. And in a unique child-pleasing service, hotel mascot Sunny the Seal will visit your villa with a bedtime snack and tuck in the kids.

Rates are $110–$180. Call (407) 352-8051 or 1-800-343-7170.

5. *The Hyatt Regency Grand Cypress Resort*

The Grand Cypress isn't a hotel, it's an event. With 750 rooms, a ½-acre pool, a 27-hole Nicklaus-designed golf course, and a 21-acre lake chock full of watercraft, you could spend a vacation here without ever leaving your hotel. (But should you decide to venture out, WDW is only 3 miles away.) Large enough to be intimidating, the Grand Cypress boasts five restaurants and a stellar Sunday brunch that's widely conceded to be the best in town, even by the staffs at other hotels.

Rates are $140–$200, and suites begin at $275. Call 1-800-228-9000.

6. *Days Inns*

If you consider a hotel merely a place to sleep, there are 21 Days Inns in the Orlando area, providing excellent value for the dollar. Rooms are $55–$70. Call 1-800-325-2525 for details and reservations.

ON THE HORIZON: PLANS FOR THE HOTELS

Disney will be aggressively moving into the 1990s with more budget and all-suite hotels.

1. Coming in 1991: Disney's Boardwalk will open between the Swan and Epcot Center, featuring live

entertainment, thrill rides, and a midway in the best Coney Island tradition. The Boardwalk Resort, an all-suite hotel with 530 units, will open later.

2. Coming in 1991: Disney's Yacht Club and Beach Club Resort, which will bring 1,214 rooms to the Epcot area, is designed to evoke images of a New England seaside resort.

3. Coming in 1991 and 1992: Disney's Port Orleans and Dixie Landings will add more than 3,000 budget-priced rooms with a Mardi Gras theme to WDW.

4. The Mediterranean Resort, on the MK monorail line with 1,000 deluxe rooms and architecture inspired by the resorts of the Greek Islands, is on its way.

5. Wilderness Lodge and Buffalo Junction, two additions to Fort Wilderness, will offer 1,300 rustic rooms in a Wild West setting.

6. Kingdom Suites Hotel will add 200 luxury suites to the Contemporary Resort and will also be on the MK monorail line.

3

★ ★ ★ ★ ★ ★ ★ ★ ★ ★ ★ ★ ★ ★ ★ ★ ★ ★ ★

Touring Plans

GENERAL WALT DISNEY WORLD TOURING TIPS

Most of the following tips assume that you'll be visiting WDW for more than 1 day. If you don't, see the 1-Day Touring Plan section.

1. *Come early!* This is the single most important piece of advice in this entire book. By beating the crowds, you can visit attractions in quick succession and also avoid the parking and transportation nightmares that occur when the parks become filled to peak capacity around 11 A.M.

For those of you with kids, it's especially important that you avoid the exhaustion that comes with just trying to get there. If you're staying off-site, it can take a full 2 hours from the point you leave your hotel to the point where you board your first ride, which is enough time to shatter the equanimity of even the best-behaved child. The kids have been waiting for this vacation a long time and flying and riding a long time, so you owe it to them to get into the parks fast.

2. On the evening you arrive, dial 824-4321 for the stated opening time of the theme park you plan to visit the next day. If you learn, for example, that the MK is scheduled to open at 9 A.M., be at the gate by 8:30. Sometimes—for no apparent reason—the gates open early, a gift from the gods that you should be prepared to capitalize on. On the mornings the park opens ahead of the stated time, you can ride a dozen attractions while the other 35,000 poor saps are still out on I-4.

3. Even if the park doesn't open ahead of the stated time, frequently guests are ushered into the first section of the park early. If this happens to you, rent strollers and get maps and entertainment schedules before entering the body of the park.

In the MK, visitors are sometimes allowed to travel the length of Main Street before the park actually opens. You can window-shop, grab a muffin at the Main Street Bakery & Cookie Shop, and still be at the ropes blocking the end of Main Street by 9 A.M., far ahead of the throngs outside the main turnstile. Similarly, at MGM, visitors are sometimes allowed onto Hollywood Boulevard to browse the shops and nibble a bite at Starring Rolls before the main park opens.

At Epcot, the advantages of an early arrival are even greater. Spaceship Earth (aka The Big Ball) is tough to get into at other times but stands silent and empty at the day's beginning. A family can get strollers, ride Spaceship Earth, make dinner reservations at the WorldKey Information Services in Earth Station, and have a quick breakfast at either the Stargate Restaurant or Sunrise Terrace Restaurant—all before the park officially opens. As an added bonus, the Disney characters, dressed in nifty spacesuits, appear in the Stargate Restaurant early in the morning and happily pose for pictures.

4. Plan to see the most popular attractions early in the day, late at night, or during a time (such as the 3 P.M. parade in the MK) where a big event siphons off other potential riders. New attractions such as the Wonders of Life pavilion in Epcot or Star Tours at MGM are always crowded, so hit these first.

Disney is expanding its hours of operation at MGM, which has drawn larger crowds than projected ever since its 1989 opening. Frequently MGM runs from 7 A.M. to midnight, even during the off-season, and attractions such as the Indiana Jones Epic Stunt Spectacular or SuperStar Television are easier to get into at night.

5. Eat at "off" times. Some families eat a huge breakfast, have a late lunch around 3 P.M., and then eat a final

meal after the parks close. Others eat lightly at breakfast, and then have lunch at 11 A.M. and dinner at 5 P.M. Families with no particular desire to try the sit-down restaurants simply snack from outdoor vendors all day.

6. Keep in mind that kids usually want to revisit their favorite attractions. (My daughter insisted on riding Dumbo every single day the first time we visited WDW, something I hadn't foreseen and which radically restructured our touring plans.) Parents who over-schedule to the point where there's no time to revisit favorites risk a mutiny.

One way to handle this problem is to leave the entire last day of your trip free as a "greatest hits" day, so that you can go back to all your favorites at least one more time. If you feel like lugging around the camcorder only once, make this the day.

7. Use the touring plan to cut down on arguments and debates. It's a hapless parent indeed who sits down at breakfast and asks "What do you want to do today?" Three kids will have three different answers, and the indecision and bickering waste valuable time. Fight your fights at home while creating the touring schedule and then stick to it.

8. When making plans, keep in mind the size of the parks. MGM is small and can be easily crisscrossed to take in various shows. The MK is larger; some cutting back and forth is possible, but you'll probably want to tour one "land" thoroughly before heading to another. Epcot is so enormous that you're almost forced to visit attractions in geographic sequence or you'll spend all your time and energy in transit.

9. If you leave a park and plan to return to either that park or another, save your stroller receipt and have your hand stamped. You won't have to pay a new

stroller deposit at the new park if you can show a receipt, and you can reenter the new park swiftly by showing your stamped hand and World Passport. (Don't
worry if you're leaving to swim—the handstamps are
waterproof.)

TOURING TIPS FOR VISITORS
STAYING ON-SITE

1. By far the greatest advantage of staying at one of
the hotels within the confines of WDW is the easy commute to the theme parks. Visitors with small kids can
return to their hotels in midafternoon and then reenter
the parks about 5 or 6 P.M. Remember the mantra:
Come early, stay late, and take a break in the middle of
the day.

If you arrive early, by 2 P.M. you'll have toured for 5 or
6 hours and be more than ready for a rest. Have a late
lunch at either one of the Main Street restaurants,
which are reasonably empty at midday, or back at your
hotel. (Neither the shuttle buses nor the monorail is
crowded in midafternoon, but if you're staying at the
Polynesian Village Resort or the Grand Floridian Resort, taking the launch or the ferryboat is even faster.)
Once "home," nap or take a dip in the pool.

At least one day you'll want to remain in the MK until
3 P.M. for the Main Street Electrical Parade. Be sure to
watch near the Railroad Station, at the Main Street
hub, so you'll be close to the main gates and able to make
a clean getaway once the parade has passed.

2. Never order breakfast through room service at a
Disney hotel. Service at the sit-down restaurants in
Disney hotels can also be maddeningly slow, so try one
of the buffet or fast-food eateries at your hotel or get
through the gates early and eat breakfast at the parks.

3. In the off-season, the MK often closes at 6 P.M. but Epcot Center and MGM stay open until 8 or 9 P.M., even during the least crowded weeks of the year. The solution? Spend mornings at the MK, return to your hotel for a break, and then spend late afternoons and evenings at Epcot or MGM. Not only does this plan buy you more hours per day in the theme parks, the best places for dinner are all at Epcot anyway.

TOURING TIPS FOR VISITORS STAYING OFF-SITE

1. Time your commute. If you can make it from your hotel to the theme park gates within 30 minutes, it may still be worth your while to return to your hotel for a midday break. This is a distinct possibility for guests at the Disney Village Hotel Plaza and some I-4 establishments. If your hotel is farther out, it's doubtful you'll want to make the drive four times a day.

2. If it isn't feasible to return to your hotel, find afternoon resting places within the parks. See the Afternoon Resting Places section in our discussions of each theme park. Sometimes kids aren't so much tired as full of pent-up energy. If you suspect that's the case, take preschoolers to the playground in Mickey's Starland (formerly Mickey's Birthdayland) in the MK or let older kids run free among the forts and backwoods paths of Tom Sawyer Island.

3. If you're willing to leave the parks in the middle of the afternoon, you have even more options. Cool off in River Country, Typhoon Lagoon, or the 10-screen movie theater beside Pleasure Island.

The hotel restaurants in the MK resorts are never crowded at lunchtime and offer much more leisurely dining than those in the parks. The monorail is slow midday, so take the ferryboat or launch to the Polynesian or Grand Floridian. A good bet is 1900 Park Fare at the Grand Floridian, which offers a buffet meal, appearances by Chip and Dale, and a giant band organ named Big Bertha.

4. If you'll be touring all day, get strollers for all preschool age kids; few 5-year-olds can walk through a 14-hour day.

5. Staying for a late evening show such as Illumi-Nations at Epcot Center or the Main Street Electrical Parade in the MK? Choose a location near the main exit so you can get the jump on the rest of the departing crowd.

6. Not staying for the late show? Leave the park while the show is in progress to miss the departing crowd altogether.

7. During the off-season, when the MK closes early, you may opt to spend your evenings at Epcot. See the 1-Day Touring for the Highly Energetic section.

HOW DO I CUSTOMIZE A TOURING PLAN?

There's no substitute for a good touring plan. Unfortunately, the generic touring schedules included in many guidebooks assume that all visitors are equally interested in all attractions, which simply isn't true. If your 7-year-old is sold on stegasophagi, for example, you may spend an entire morning in the Universe of Energy pavilion at Epcot. On the other hand, if no one in your group likes anything remotely scary, you can cross certain attractions off your list from the start.

In creating a personalized touring plan, step 1 is to

familiarize yourself with the overall map of WDW and the maps of the three major theme parks so you can arrive in Orlando with some sense of proximity and the location of major attractions. Getting to Big Thunder Mountain Railroad early is considerably easier if you know where Big Thunder Mountain Railroad is. Next, poll your family on which attractions they most want to see, and build these priorities into the plan.

Step 3 is to divide each day of your visit into three components: morning, afternoon, and evening. You don't have to specify where you'll be every hour—that's too confining—but you need some sense of how you'll break up each day. Check out the following plan, which is an adaptation of The Perfect Touring Plan for 4- or 5-Day Visits section described later. This plan is custom-designed for a family with a 3-year-old girl and a 7-year-old boy who'll be at WDW for 4 days in October, staying at the on-site Caribbean Beach Resort. The younger child adores the characters and most yearns to meet Minnie Mouse up close and in person. She still naps in the afternoon. The older child likes action rides, is pretty fearless when it comes to special effects, and especially wants to see The Living Seas at Epcot Center. The husband asks only that one afternoon be left open for golfing. The wife would like some time in the parks without the kids to get an early jump on Christmas shopping and wants to get a sitter one evening for a parents' night out.

A touring plan for this family might look something like this:

Wednesday am:	Magic Kingdom—tour Fantasyland, Mickey's Starland, and Tomorrowland.
Wednesday pm:	Return to hotel for lunch and naps around 2 P.M.

Wednesday nt:	Epcot—tour Future World, including The Living Seas.
Thursday am:	Disney-MGM Studios Theme Park.
Thursday pm:	Return to hotel around 3 P.M. Mom supervises swimming and naps while dad golfs.
Thursday nt:	Hoop-Dee-Doo Musical Revue at Fort Wilderness Campground Resort; afterward watch Electrical Water Pageant on the lagoon.
Friday am:	MK—Ride Big Thunder Mountain Railroad first, then tour Adventureland, Liberty Square, and Frontierland. Lunch late in the park at Cinderella Castle and then take in the 3 P.M. parade.
Friday pm:	While dad takes kids back for swim and rest, mom stays behind to shop.
Friday nt:	Sitter comes to hotel room for kids while mom and dad eat at Bistro de Paris in Epcot.
Saturday am:	Return to MK and reride all the favorites.
Saturday pm:	Lunch at the Mexico pavilion at Epcot. Tour the World Showcase, encouraging kids to rest and/or nap during films since this is the only day you won't be returning to your room for an afternoon nap. Meet Disney characters at 5 P.M. show near the lagoon.
Saturday nt:	Dinner at the Coral Reef Restaurant. Then tour the rest of Future World and see IllumiNations.

Sunday am: Take in a character breakfast at the
                        Polynesian Village Resort. Return
                        to room, pack, and leave before the
                        11 A.M. checkout time. Head for
                        airport.

This touring plan has much to recommend it:

1. You can get an early start every day.
2. Naps or at least downtime is built into the afternoon.
3. You see the characters every day.
4. Minimal time is spent waiting in lines. Certain
   reservations, such as those for the Hoop-Dee-Doo
   Musical Revue and character breakfast at the
   Polynesian Village Resort, can be made before you
   leave home. Other reservations, such as dinner for
   two at Bistro de Paris and the final dinner meal at
   the Coral Reef Restaurant, can be made from your
   hotel room.

THE PERFECT TOURING PLAN
FOR 4- OR 5-DAY VISITS

This is the ideal length for a WDW visit. *Note:* Even if
you plan to tour the WDW parks for only 4 days, a 5-day
World Passport may still be a better buy since it admits
visitors to Pleasure Island, Discovery Island, Typhoon
Lagoon, and River Country as well as the three major
parks.

  This touring plan puts you in more than one theme
park almost every day, thus avoiding It's a Small World
burnout and endless debates over whether a day is better spent in the MK or Epcot.

Day 1

Be at the end of Main Street in the MK by the stated opening time. When the ropes drop (assuming that your kids are 7 or older and game for it), head directly for Space Mountain.

After you ride Space Mountain, go to Fantasyland. (If your children are younger or frightened by coasters, go to Fantasyland first.) If you want to eat lunch inside the castle, make your reservation at King Stefan's Banquet Hall now. Ride these Fantasyland rides in rapid succession:

Dumbo, the Flying Elephant

Cinderella's Golden Carrousel

Snow White's Adventures

Peter Pan's Flight

It's a Small World

Mr. Toad's Wild Ride (optional)

20,000 Leagues Under the Sea (optional)

Mad Tea Party (optional)

After you exit the Tea Party teeter, on to Mickey's Starland. The kids can enjoy the petting zoo and playground while you wait for the next show. (Starland is also one of the best places in the park to take pictures.)

When the show is concluded and you've met Mickey, stop for a snack before you head toward Adventureland because it's a fairly far walk.

In Adventureland, visit Pirates of the Caribbean, the Jungle Cruise, and the Swiss Family Treehouse. By now it should be midday, and some of the lines may be prohibitive. If you face a wait of more than 25 minutes, skip that attraction. You'll need to be back out on Main

Street by 2 P.M., and you'll be returning to the MK on other days.

As you exit Adventureland around 2 P.M. and head toward Main Street, stop at the Crystal Palace, Plaza Restaurant, or Tony's and eat a hearty lunch. (If you've made lunch reservations for King Stefan's Banquet Hall, go there now.)

Watch the 3 P.M. character parade from the Main Street hub.

After the parade, exit the theme park. It's now time for your well-deserved midday break. Be sure to have your hand stamped as you exit the park.

About 6 or 7 P.M., go to MGM. Pick up an entertainment schedule at Guest Services as you enter. You should easily be able to catch the Indiana Jones Epic Stunt Spectacular, SuperStar Television, and the Animation Tour and eat at one of the fast-food places before 11 P.M.

Enjoy the 11 P.M. fireworks presentation. (Times for this finale show vary, so consult your entertainment schedule.)

Day 2

Be through the MK gates early. This time when the ropes drop, hoof it to Big Thunder Mountain Railroad.

While in Frontierland, see the Country Bear Vacation Hoedown, and then tour the Haunted Mansion in Liberty Square.

If you missed any Adventureland or Fantasyland attractions the previous day, tour them now. If the kids are restless, you might opt to visit Tom Sawyer Island

and have a snack at Aunt Polly's Landing while they explore.

Be on the Main Street side of Cinderella Castle for the 12:30 character show. (Starting times vary, so consult your entertainment schedule.)

Exit the park and take an early midday break. Eat lunch while you're out of the park.

Enter Epcot about 4:30 P.M. If you're staying at an on-site hotel, you should have made a dinner reservation in advance. If not, stop by the WorldKey Information Services in Earth Station and see which restaurants still have seating times left.

You may have time to catch the 5 P.M. character show at the World Showcase Lagoon.

Tour The Living Seas, The Land, and Journey into Imagination and see *Captain EO,* the hugely popular 3-D film starring Michael Jackson. Eat dinner and be at the Mexico or Canada pavilion for the closing presentation of IlluniNations.

Day 3

Start your day at MGM. Take in The Great Movie Ride and Star Tours immediately upon entering the park. Then make lunch reservations at the 50's Prime Time Cafe and head for the Backstage Studio Tour.

After the tour concludes, have lunch and then visit the Muppets and the Monster Sound show. Exit the park in midafternoon and return to your hotel for swimming, boating, sunning, and resting.

This is parents' night out. You should have arranged a sitter in advance. Orlando has many elegant restaurants (some of them inside Epcot), or you may prefer a rowdier evening at Pleasure Island.

Day 4

Start your day early at Epcot. With any luck, you should be able to make lunch reservations and tour Spaceship Earth before the ropes are dropped.

Head straight for the new and popular Wonders of Life pavilion. Ride Body Wars first, and then proceed to *Cranium Command* and *The Making of Me*.

Tour Horizons and World of Motion.

Head toward the World Showcase Lagoon.

Ride El Rio del Tiempo: The River of Time in Mexico and Maelstrom in Norway, and then have lunch in either the Mexico or Norway pavilion.

Continue circling the World Showcase Lagoon. The presentations at the China, France, and Canada pavilions and The American Adventure are all compelling and extremely well done, as are the comedy street shows in Italy and the United Kingdom. Take in as many of these as time and your child's stamina permit. Finish with the Universe of Energy pavilion on your way out of the park.

Exit Epcot Center. Enjoy a midday rest.

You should have made reservations for the Hoop-Dee-Doo Musical Revue in advance. After taking in the show, you may want to watch the Electrical Water Pageant from the beach at Fort Wilderness Campground Resort.

Day 5

Start the day with one of the character breakfasts. If you're booked on an early flight or face a long drive home, check out after you eat.

If you have a fifth day in the parks, make this round-up day, returning to visit anything you missed or re-visiting favorites.

1-DAY TOURING PLAN

If you're going to be in WDW only 1 day, your task is challenging indeed. Your 1-day ticket entitles you to entrance to only one theme park, so select carefully. Time will be at a premium, so you'll probably want to forgo your midday break, opting instead for finding afternoon resting places inside the theme park.

1. If you only have 1 day, it's imperative that you're at the park and through the gates a half hour before the stated opening time. (At the MK, with its convoluted transportation system, this means leaving your hotel 1 hour to 1 hour and 15 minutes before the park's stated opening time.)

2. Turn to the section of this book that refers to your theme park and read the "Spending Your First Hour in . . ." discussion (pages 62, 92, and 117).

3. See as many attractions as possible in the morning, moving swiftly from one to the next. If any attraction has a line requiring more than a half-hour wait, skip it for now. You can try it again just before park closing, when lines are usually much shorter.

4. Have lunch, and then move on to theater-style attractions that allow you to sit, or consult the Afternoon Resting Places section of this book.

5. The parades and character shows in mid- to late afternoon are quite worthwhile.

6. About 6 P.M., crowds thin out a bit. Eat a snack supper and then return to any sections of the park you

missed or that had long lines earlier. Save the most popular attraction for last.

7. Park closing. One parent should stake out a spot as near as possible to the main exit to watch the closing festivities while the other parent takes the kids to pick out a souvenir. It may also be a good time to grab a dessert or ice cream while waiting for the parade/fireworks/laser show to begin.

8. As soon as the closing festivities conclude, head directly out of the park. Don't look back—the crowds behind you will be the scariest thing you've seen all day.

1-DAY TOURING FOR THE HIGHLY ENERGETIC

Following is an eclectic but efficient touring plan for families (1) with a multiday World Passport (2) who are staying off-site and (3) driving their own car.

1. Epcot is much easier to get to by car than the Magic Kingdom. Early-arriving visitors can park very close to the main entry gate and simply walk in, often circumventing even the need for a tram.

2. Drive to Epcot at least 30 minutes before the stated opening time, get strollers and maps, and make your evening dinner reservation at the WorldKey Information Services in Earth Station. Have breakfast if you haven't eaten, and ride Spaceship Earth.

3. Tour Future World until about 11 A.M., and then exit Epcot, turning in your stroller and keeping the receipt. Take the monorail to the TTC and transfer to the MK monorail. You'll be running just behind the surge of visitors that usually glut the MK main gates between 10 and 11 A.M. Use

your receipt to get a new stroller at MK and have lunch on Main Street.

4. Tour the MK until 2:45. Return to the Main Street hub and watch the 3 P.M. parade.

5. Exit the MK immediately after the parade. Again, monorail traffic should be light since most MK visitors are still watching the parade snake its way through the rest of the route. Go back to the TTC and take the monorail to Epcot. You should be back there in time for the 5 P.M. character show at the World Showcase Lagoon. Then eat at the Epcot restaurant for which you made your reservations that morning, and tour the World Showcase until the closing presentation of IllumiNations.

6. After IllumiNations is over, you'll feel mighty smug as you bypass the horrendous crowds in line for the monorails and parking trams. Walk to your car and exit the park.

This touring plan admittedly calls for a lot of energy and probably shouldn't be attempted by families with preschoolers since they'll be going at full gallop for 14 hours. But this plan also lets you see three major presentations, do a bit of touring at two of the three major parks, and eat at an Epcot restaurant, which is quite a bit to accomplish in a single day.

4

★ ★ ★ ★ ★ ★ ★ ★ ★ ★ ★ ★ ★ ★ ★ ★ ★ ★ ★

The Magic Kingdom

MAGIC KINGDOM

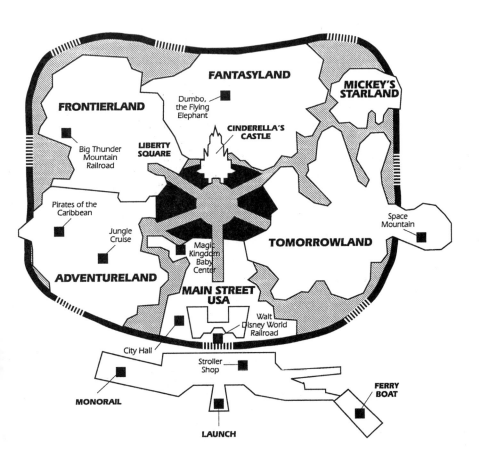

GETTING TO THE MAGIC KINGDOM

1. If you're staying off-site or at Fort Wilderness Campground Resort, the Walt Disney World Swan or Dolphin, the Caribbean Beach Resort, or The Disney Inn, prepare for a complicated journey. Either drive or take a shuttle bus to the TTC. From the TTC you can cross the Seven Seas Lagoon by ferryboat or monorail and then enter the front gates. The turnstiles to the right are usually less crowded than those to the left.

2. If you're staying at the Contemporary Resort, you can bypass the TTC and take the monorail directly to the MK.

3. If you're staying at the Grand Floridian Resort, the monorail will have you at the MK within minutes, or you can take the launch from the marina dock.

4. Guests at the Polynesian Village Resort have the most choices: the launch, the monorail, or the ferryboat. If your room is on the lagoon, walk to the ferryboat. If you're staying in one of the buildings near the Great Ceremonial House, the monorail is a better bet. If your room is close to the pool, take the launch.

When leaving at the end of the day, if you're staying off-site, pause for a second as you exit the gates. A ferryboat is the fastest route back to the TTC, but if there's no boat in sight, you're better off queuing up for the monorail.

If you're staying at the Contemporary, exit via the monorail.

If you're staying at the Polynesian or the Grand Floridian, glance down at the launch dock, which is straight ahead as you exit the MK gates. If a launch is in the dock, take it back to your hotel; otherwise, head for the monorail.

GETTING AROUND THE MAGIC KINGDOM

Walking is by far the fastest means of transport in the MK. The trolleys, vintage cars, and horse-drawn carriages are fun, as is the railroad that makes stops on Main Street, in Frontierland, and in Mickey's Starland. But consider the trolleys, trains, and skyways as pleasant rides offering charming views, not as a serious means of getting around the park.

Be prepared to make frequent rest stops while touring the MK. You won't walk as much as you do in Epcot, but you're likely to spend more time waiting in lines. Standing still is ultimately harder on the feet—and the nerves—than walking.

SPENDING YOUR FIRST HOUR
IN THE MAGIC KINGDOM

1. Be through the gates 20 minutes earlier than the stated opening time, 40 if you plan to have breakfast on Main Street. Get strollers, pick up a map and entertainment schedule at City Hall, and, if you want, make reservations for The Diamond Horseshow Jamboree (at Frontierland) at the Hospitality House.

2. Be at the end of Main Street by the stated opening time. When the ropes drop, head for Space Mountain, Big Thunder Mountain Railroad, or the Jungle Cruise if your kids are 7 or older.

3. If your kids are 6 or younger, head straight through Cinderella Castle to Fantasyland. When most people reach the end of Main Street, they tend to veer left toward Adventureland or right toward Tomorrowland and thus begin touring in a clockwise or counterclockwise fashion. If you go straight to Fantasyland now, you'll not only be able to tour five or six attractions before 10 A.M., you'll also spend the rest of your day moving against the crowds.

4. If there's a gap in the ages of your children—say the 9-year-old is ready for Space Mountain but the 4-year-old isn't—split up. Mom can take one child, dad the other, and you can meet up again in 1 hour.

MAIN STREET TOURING TIPS

1. Don't stop to savor the shops or minor attractions of Main Street in the morning—you need to hurry on to the big rides.

2. Return to Main Street to shop in midafternoon. Especially worthwhile are Disney Clothiers, Uptown Jewelers, and The Emporium. Main Street is also a good place for lunch.

3. Take a midafternoon rest (about 2 P.M., just prior to the parade) with toddlers and babies in The Walt Disney Story. Older kids still raring to go can visit the Penny Arcade and meet you later.

4. After shopping, stow your purchases in the lockers underneath the railroad. If you're not planning to see the parade, be sure to be off Main Street by 2:30 P.M. because after that time it's a mob scene.

FANTASYLAND TOURING TIPS

1. Visit Fantasyland before 11 A.M., after 5 P.M., or during the 3 P.M. parade.

2. Don't eat or shop in Fantasyland. Similar food and toys can be found elsewhere in far less crowded areas of the MK.

3. Park your strollers in one spot and walk from ride to ride. Fantasyland is geographically small, so walking is easier than constantly loading and re-loading the kids in strollers to push them only a few steps.

4. Dumbo, the Flying Elephant and Cinderella's Golden Carrousel can have long lines, and both rides load slowly. The waiting areas are completely exposed to the sun, which can be sweltering for an adult and even worse for 3-year-olds. One parent should stand in line while the other grabs a Coke with the kids. As the queue makes its last turn before boarding, simply hand the kids over to the parent who has been waiting in line.

5. The Disney characters sometimes appear at the base of Cinderella Castle, but this is the worst place in WDW to see them. Try Mickey's Starland or, better yet, Epcot.

FANTASYLAND

The aptly named Fantasyland, located directly behind Cinderella Castle, is a cross between a Bavarian village and a medieval fair. Most of the kiddie rides are here, so it's the most congested section of the MK.

Fantasyland Attractions

It's a Small World

During this 11-minute boat ride, dolls representing children of all nations greet you with a song so infectious that you'll be humming it at bedtime. *Note:* Although the lines look intimidating, they move fast. This is one of the best of all attractions to film with a VCR.

Peter Pan's Flight

Tinkerbell flutters overhead as you board miniature pirate ships and sail above Nana's doghouse, the sparkling night streets of London, the Indian camp, and Captain Hook's cove. Of all the MK attractions, this one is most true to the movie that inspired it. Since the re-release of *Peter Pan* in 1989, the attraction is more popular than ever.

Skyway to Tomorrowland

This overhead cable car is great for the view, but as a mode of transport, forget it—walking's faster.

Magic Journeys

An 8-minute 3-D film with startlingly lifelike effects. Kids unfamiliar with the 3-D concept love the glasses and giggle insanely as kites and balloons appear to drift out toward the audience. *Note:* One of the few places in Fantasyland designed for resting.

Mr. Toad's Wild Ride

Cars careen through a funhouse, narrowly missing a chicken coop and an oncoming train and being crushed by a teetering grandfather clock. *Note:* Although the special effects are nowhere near up to the standard of Peter Pan's Flight, younger kids may enjoy it.

Cinderella's Golden Carrousel

Seventy-two white horses prance while a pipe organ toots out "Chim-Chim-Cheree" and other Disney classics. *Note:* Gorgeous at night. Benches nearby let mom and dad take a breather.

Snow White's Adventures

You ride mining cars through the dark, and a wicked witch appears several times quite suddenly and drops a boulder on you at the end. Although the ride isn't really scary, a few toddlers get the willies. The acid test is: How well did your kids handle the scene in the movie when Snow White is chased through the forest? My 4-year-old liked the ride while she was on it but, significantly, didn't want to try it again the next day.

Note: Snow White herself is nowhere to be seen. Families expecting a happy retelling of the movie story are in for a shock.

20,000 Leagues Under the Sea

This submarine ride features sunken treasure, octopi, and other marine life, culminating in an attack by a giant squid.

Note: The ride boards slowly and doesn't compare to the real-life adventures of The Living Seas at Epcot. Unless the queues are short, skip it.

Dumbo, the Flying Elephant

This happy little elephant has become the center of some controversy: Is he worth the wait or not? Although the lines do indeed move slowly, making a 1-hour wait for a 90-second ride possible, there's something special about this attraction. It's frequently featured in the ads, so it has become an integral part of our collective Disney consciousness, and since riders make Dumbo fly by pressing a button, it's one of only two Fantasyland rides that aren't totally passive. *Note:* Go for it. If you aren't the sort of person willing to invest an hour of agony for 90 seconds of joy, you probably shouldn't have had children in the first place.

Mad Tea Party

Spinning pastel cups, propelled by their riders, swirl around the Soused Mouse, who periodically pops out of the teapot. Since the rider largely controls how fast the teacup spins, visitors of all ages can enjoy this ride.

Note: Rider volume ebbs and flows at this attraction. If the line looks too daunting, grab a drink at the nearby Tomorrowland Terrace; by the time you emerge, the crowd may have dispersed.

Mickey's Starland (Formerly Mickey's Birthdayland)

More like a single, unified attraction than a land, Mickey's Starland was opened in 1989. Mickey's house dominates the miniature town of Duckburg, which also contains an unassuming petting zoo and playground. But the main attraction is a musical stage show celebrating Mickey's 60th birthday.

To get to the party, wander through Mickey's memorabilia-crammed house and on to the preshow tent, where cartoons and life-sized cutouts of Disney movie stills are on hand to amuse the kids while you await the main event. Approximately every 25 minutes guests are ushered into the Birthday Theater, where the characters present a lively, kid-pleasing show.

As Minnie plans Mickey's surprise party, she receives a lot of well-intentioned help from the other characters, including Pluto, who's determined to drop his bone into the cake batter. Unlike at other Disney shows, here you sit quite close to the stage, and everyone gets into the action, shouting out warnings when Pluto sneaks toward the mixing bowl, happily screaming when the oven explodes.

The show culminates with the arrival of Mickey and a rousing rendition of "Happy Birthday" while the characters dance on a 10-foot cake. As the characters are hitting their last note, prepare to exit via the doors to your left and head for Mickey's Hollywood Theater, which is next door to the party tent. Many people think that the party is the end of the show and leave without realizing that they can visit Mickey in his personal dressing room. If you exit promptly now, you'll be the first in line.

Guests are taken in groups of 10 to meet Mickey. This is by far your best chance in all of WDW to meet the main mouse since Disney zealously guards Mickey's star status by having him appear around the theme parks less frequently than the other characters, and for shorter periods of time. Families who've toured several days without yet snagging that obligatory picture of the kids posing with Mickey are almost in tears of gratitude as they enter the dressing room.

Mickey's Starland is a must if your kids are under 7, probably skippable for others. Also, be advised that you can meet Mickey without taking in the birthday party: Just go straight to the Hollywood Theater and get in line.

Note: The WDW railroad that stops on Main Street and in Frontierland also drops off guests at Mickey's Starland. The ride is designed to get kids in a festive party mood—sometimes Goofy chases the train and just misses getting aboard, and riders pass a deserted tea party, indicating that Alice and the Mad Hatter are also on their way to Starland. But arriving by train is no faster than walking, and in fact, since you detrain with a couple of hundred other partygoers who all swarm the birthday tent en masse, it may even waste time. If your kids are young and you visit Starland two or three times, try the train once, but be aware that it isn't the only way to get to the party.

TOMORROWLAND TOURING TIPS

1. If you plan on riding Space Mountain, make a beeline there immediately after entering the front gates. From 9:30 A.M. on there are substantial lines.

2. If you don't plan on riding Space Mountain, save Tomorrowland for early afternoon touring, when the park is at its most crowded. Several Tomorrowland attractions (American Journeys, Mission to Mars, and Carousel of Progress) are high-capacity and relatively easy to get into even during the most crowded times in the park. Others (WEDway PeopleMover, Dreamflight) are similarly easy to board and give you the added bonus of letting you sit a while.

3. If you're looking for fast food during peak dining hours, Tomorrowland food stands are never as busy as those in the other areas of the park.

TOMORROWLAND

A precursor to Epcot, and looking a bit dated in comparison, Tomorrowland has relatively few attractions that appeal to children under 7. With the exception of the area around Space Mountain, Tomorrowland is the least crowded section of the MK.

Tomorrowland Attractions

Space Mountain

This 3-minute roller-coaster ride through inky darkness is the sole scream ripper in the MK. The cars move at "only" 28 mph, a fairly tame pace compared to that of the monster coasters at some theme parks, but the special effects are extremely convincing. Space Mountain is the most popular MK attraction with visitors 7–21.

Children under 7 must have an adult present to ride. Children under 3 and pregnant women are prohibited. Some kids 3–7 loved the ride, but most surveyed found it too scary. Only you know if your children are up to this attraction.

Grand Prix Raceway

These tiny sports cars, which any child over 4 feet 4 inches tall can drive, circle a nifty-looking miniature racetrack. Unfortunately, this is one attraction that looks far more fun than it is. Car-crazed kids enjoy the ride, but many people find the cars pokey and the raceway boring. If you're on a tight schedule, skip it.

Skyway to Fantasyland

The skyway offers a pretty view, especially at night, but by the time you wait in line to board, you could've walked.

Delta Dreamflight

This is a happy, upbeat ride tracing the history of flight. It's not terribly special, at least not in comparison to similar Epcot attractions, but it loads quickly and preschoolers like it.

Starjets

This circular thrill ride, a sort of Dumbo on steroids, is a bit too much for preschoolers and a bit too little for teens. Kids 7–11 rated it highly; children of other ages should skip it.

CircleVision 360 American Journeys

This is the original Disney 360-degree CircleVision film, featuring breathtaking footage of the Grand Canyon, the Florida Keys, the Statue of Liberty, and other U.S. vacation destinations. The film is extremely well done. Unfortunately, guests stand throughout the presentation and strollers aren't allowed inside the theater, which means that babies and toddlers have to be held during the 30-minute show, a condition that eliminates the attraction for many families.

Carousel of Progress

Another forerunner to the type of technology now on display at Epcot Center, Carousel was one of the first Disney Audio-Animatronic shows, and it demonstrates how the life of the average American family has been improved through electricity. Large crowds can enter at once, so it's a good choice for midafternoon.

WEDway PeopleMover

This little tram-train circles Tomorrowland and provides fun views, including a glimpse inside Space Mountain.

Mission to Mars

Young kids may be put off by the rumblings and loud noises of this simulated shuttle flight to Mars. The seats inside the round cabin quake and shake during lift-off, but the final film footage showing the surface of the red planet is impressive. A large digital clock outside the attraction keeps you posted as to waiting time. Another good choice for midafternoon.

ADVENTURELAND, FRONTIERLAND, AND LIBERTY SQUARE TOURING TIPS

1. On your second morning in the MK, begin your touring day in Frontierland, at Big Thunder Mountain Railroad. Then backtrack to Adventureland and ride the Jungle Cruise and Pirates of the Caribbean. All three attractions are a snap to board before 10 A.M., and you can return to ride less-crowded Adventureland and Frontierland attractions later in the day.

2. Because most visitors tour the lands in a clockwise or counterclockwise fashion, these three lands reach peak capacity about noon and stay crowded until 4 P.M. or so, when the people lined up to watch the 3 P.M. parade finally disperse. So if you miss the Jungle Cruise or Big Thunder Mountain Railroad in the morning, wait until early evening to revisit them.

3. Should you, despite your best intentions, wind up in one of these three sections in midafternoon, you'll find a bit of breathing space on Tom Sawyer Island, with The Enchanted Tiki Birds or among the shops in the shady Adventureland pavilion. Surprisingly, Pirates of the Caribbean isn't that difficult to board in midafternoon. The lines look terrible, but at least you wait inside, and this is one of the fastest-loading attractions in WDW.

ADVENTURELAND

Thematically the most bizarre of all the lands, sort of a "Bourbon Street meets Trinidad by way of the Congo," Adventureland still manages to effectively convey an exotic mood.

Adventureland Attractions

Jungle Cruise

You'll meet up with headhunters, hyenas, water-spewing elephants, and other varieties of frankly fake wildlife on this 10-minute boat ride. What distinguishes this attraction is the hilarious patter of the tour guides—these young men in pith helmets are unsung heroes of Disney casting genius.

The cruise isn't very scary, is fun for all, and the lines move with agonizing slowness. Go in the morning.

The Swiss Family Treehouse

A real split of opinion here—some visitors love this replica of the ultimate treehouse, others rate it as dull. One word of warning: This is a tough attraction to tour with toddlers. The steps are numerous, and at times the climbing is a bit too precarious for unsteady little legs. Lugging a 2-year-old through the exhibit is tiring, but the real problem is that the bamboo and rigging look so enticing kids that want to climb on their own, and at their own pace, which won't sit well with the 800 people in line behind you.

The Enchanted Tiki Birds, aka Tropical Serenade

Interestingly, these singing/talking birds, and the singing/talking flowers and statues around them, represent

Disney's first attempt at the Audio-Animatronics that are now such an integral part of Epcot magic. Like the treehouse, this attraction draws a wide range of ratings, but the show is amusing and does move fast. Perhaps most importantly, the Tiki birds do their stuff in an air-conditioned theater.

Pirates of the Caribbean
The Pirates inspire great loyalty, and a significant number of guests of all ages name this ride as their favorite in all the MK. Your boat goes over a small waterfall, and there's a bit of menace on the faces of some buccaneers, but few kids leave the Pirates frightened. Most would agree with the 5-year-old who voted the ride "best reason to leave Fantasyland."

FRONTIERLAND

Kids love the rough-and-tumble Wild West feel of Frontierland, which is home of several of the MK's most popular attractions.

Frontierland Attractions

Big Thunder Mountain Railroad
A roller coaster disguised as a runaway mine train, Big Thunder is considerably less scary than Space Mountain, but almost as popular. The glory of the ride is in the setting: You zoom through a deserted mining town populated with bats, rainmakers, and saloon denizens, all crafted Disney style.

If you're wondering if the coaster may be too much for your kids, be advised that Big Thunder Mountain Railroad is more in the rattle-back-and-forth than the lose-your-stomach-as-you-plunge tradition. Almost any child over 7 should be able to handle the dips and twists; preschoolers are iffier; see how they react to the Pirates of the Caribbean or the Maelstrom rides in Epcot's Norway pavilion first.

Note: Children under 7 must ride with an adult, and no one shorter than 40 inches is allowed to board.

Diamond Horseshoe Jamboree

Sandwiches and punch are served during this 30-minute saloon show, which is full of hokey humor and lively dancing. Some of the puns will go over the heads of younger children, but the material is delivered in the same broad style as the Hoop-Dee-Doo Musical Revue, so kids find themselves laughing even when they're not quite sure why.

Make reservations for the jamboree at the Hospitality House as you enter in the morning. Between standing in line, eating, and the show, you'll end up devoting over an hour to the jamboree. That may be an advantage if you have young kids who nap, if you're pregnant, or if you just want a midday place to rest, but it's a disadvantage if you're on a tight touring schedule. See the jamboree only if (1) you'll be in the MK for more than 1 day and (2) you aren't planning to see the similar Hoop-Dee-Doo Musical Revue at Fort Wilderness Campground Resort.

Frontierland Shootin' Arcade

Bring your quarters. This is a pretty standard shooting gallery but a good place for the kids to kill a few minutes while adults wait in line at the Country Bear Vacation Hoedown.

Country Bear Vacation Hoedown

Kids of all ages fall for the funny, furry Audio-Animatronic's critters featured in this 15-minute show. From the coy Teddi Barra to the incomparable Big Al, from Bubbles, Bunny, and Beulah (a sort of combination of the Andrews Sisters and the Beach Boys) to Melvin the Moosehead, each face is distinctive and lovable.

The hoedown is extremely popular, but sometimes you can slip in during the 3 P.M. parade. (But don't, for heaven's sake, try to get in just after the parade, when thousands of tourists suddenly find themselves on the streets of Frontierland with nothing to do.) This is also an excellent attraction to visit in the last hour before closing.

Tom Sawyer Island

A getaway playground full of caves, bridges, forts, and windmills, Tom Sawyer Island is a good destination when the kids become too rambunctious to handle. Adults can sip a lemonade at Aunt Polly's Landing, the island fast-food restaurant, while the kids run free.

The one drawback is that the island is accessible only by raft, which means you often have to wait to get there and wait to get back. If your kids are under 5, don't bother making the trip because the terrain is too rough and widespread for preschoolers to play without supervision; young kids can better blow off steam at the playground in Mickey's Starland. But if your kids are 5–9 and beginning to resemble wild Indians, stop off at Tom Sawyer Island, where such behavior is not only acceptable but de rigueur.

Davy Crockett Explorer Canoes

Like the riverboat and keelboats of Liberty Square, these crafts circle the Rivers of America around Tom Sawyer Island, affording you unusual views of Big

Thunder Mountain Railroad and the other sights of Frontierland. Unlike the riverboat and keelboats, however, the canoes are human-powered, which makes them appealing to some tourists, appalling to others. Don't board unless you're prepared to row.

Note: The canoes are in dock only during the summer and major holidays.

LIBERTY SQUARE

Walk on a few feet from Frontierland and you'll find yourself transported back 100 years, to Colonial America, strolling the cobblestone streets of Liberty Square.

Liberty Square Attractions

Liberty Square Riverboat

The second tier of this paddle wheel riverboat offers outstanding views of Liberty Square and Frontierland, but, as with the other Rivers of America crafts, board only if you have a time to kill and the boat is in the dock. *Note:* There are some seats, but most riders stand.

The Hall of Presidents

This attraction may remind you that one of the villains in the movie *The Stepford Wives* was a Disney engineer. The Hall of Presidents is indeed a Stepford version of the presidency, with eerily lifelike and quietly dignified chief executives, each responding to his name during the roll call with a nod or tilting of the head. In the background, other presidents fidget and whisper.

The presidential roll call and the film on the Constitution that precedes it will probably bore kids under 10.

Older children will find the 20-minute presentation educational, if not particularly awe-inspiring. (This attraction may help assuage your guilt if you've taken the children out of school for the trip.) Babies and toddlers find the hall a fine place to nap.

Note: The theater holds up to 700 people, which means that lines disappear every 25 minutes. Ask one of the attendants at the lobby doors how long it is before the next show, and amble in about 10 minutes before showtime.

Mike Fink Keel Boats

These small boats follow the same route as the canoes and riverboat. But the riverboat holds more people at a time, so if you want to try out one of the three watercrafts, the riverboat is a better choice.

The Haunted Mansion

More apt to elicit a giggle than a scream, the mansion is full of clever special effects. (See The Scare Factor at the Magic Kingdom section.) The cast members, who dress as morticians and never smile, add considerably to the fun with such instructions as "Drag your wretched bodies to the dead center of the room." A significant number of kids 7–11 listed The Haunted Mansion as one of their favorite attractions.

The mansion is best viewed before noon, or—if you have the courage—in the last 2 hours before closing.

FULL-SERVICE RESTAURANTS IN THE MAGIC KINGDOM

1. *Tony's* (Formerly The Town Square Cafe)   Located in the Main Street Hub

This thoroughly enjoyable restaurant is dedicated to *Lady and the Tramp,* with scenes from the popular Disney film dotting the walls and a statue of the canine romantics in the center. The cuisine, like that of the cafe where Tramp wooed Lady, is classic Italian, and the portions are generous.

Tony's is a terrific choice for breakfast because, along with the other Main Street eateries, it begins serving ½ hour before the park officially opens. The Mickey character waffles are real kid pleasers, as are most of the offerings on the kiddie menu. The menus, which are full of pictures of Lady and the Tramp to color, are handed out with crayons, and the wait at Tony's is never long, making it a good choice for families with toddlers in tow. It's moderately priced and open for breakfast, lunch, and dinner.

2. *Plaza Restaurant*   Located on Main Street

The Plaza has a relaxing setting, and the sandwiches, quiche, and chef's salads are very filling. Try the chicken pot pie, which is encased in a huge pastry puff, or the milkshakes, which are trotted over from the Sealtest Ice Cream Parlor next door. The Plaza is moderately priced and open for lunch and dinner.

3. *Crystal Palace*   Located between Main Street and Adventureland

The MK's only cafeteria offers something for everyone and allows picky eaters a chance to pick. You can find a classic eggs and bacon breakfast here, salads and sandwiches at lunch, and nearly anything you please at dinner, even that most elusive of all MK foods, vegetables. And the setting is absolutely lovely.

One warning: Because of its central location and distinctive architecture, few visitors pass by the Crystal Palace without checking it out. The cafeteria is especially crowded from noon to 2 P.M., so you should aim to go around 11 A.M. or in midafternoon. The Crystal Palace is moderately priced and open for breakfast, lunch, and dinner.

4. *Liberty Tree Tavern*   Located in Liberty Square
Crammed with antiques and decorated in a style reminiscent of Colonial Williamsburg, the tavern serves salads and sandwiches at lunch, along with more than passable clam chowder. The dinner menu offers prime rib, seafood, and chicken. Reservations are recommended, but, unlike King Stefan's Banquet Hall, no one is at the door to take them until 11 A.M. Either plan to eat early, when you can usually walk in without a reservation, or make reservations as you leave Fantasyland midmorning. The Tavern is moderately expensive and open for lunch and dinner.

5. *King Stefan's Banquet Hall*   Located in Cinderella Castle, Fantasyland
Nestled high amid the spires of the castle, this restaurant—named, mysteriously enough, for Sleeping Beauty's father—is very popular. Make reservations at the restaurant door first thing in the morning, but even with reservations you can expect to wait for both your table and food. Because the service is slow and the menu pricey, King Stefan's isn't a place to drop into casually.

Is it worth it? Yes, if your kids like Cinderella. The first time I ever visited the MK with my daughter, we booked lunch at King Stefan's, hoping to catch a mere glimpse of Leigh's idol, unaware that Cinderella herself often greets diners at the door. An elevator lifted us and other diners to the second story of the castle. When the doors opened to reveal Cinderella in all her glory, Leigh's knees buckled. For a second I honestly thought she'd fainted. "Welcome to my castle," Cinderella cooed, as I grabbed Leigh under the armpits and dragged her to our table. She spent the meal in shock, refusing to eat and her eyes never leaving Cinderella as she moved among the tables posing for pictures and autographing the distinctive pumpkin-shaped kiddie menus.

So King Stefan's does have an irresistibly romantic appeal for young diners. The setting of the high-ceiling massive banquet hall is spectacular, and the lead glass windows overlook the rides of Fantasyland. King Stefan's also offers a relatively ambitious menu, including a gorgeous fruit plate and yummy prime rib sandwiches. The desserts are as stunning as the view. The restaurant is expensive and open for lunch and dinner.

DECENT FAST-FOOD PLACES IN THE MAGIC KINGDOM

1. The Mile Long Bar in Frontierland is a good place for Tex-Mex foods, and the lines move more swiftly than those at the Pecos Bill Cafe next door.

2. Tomorrowland Terrace is by far the fastest of the hamburger and fries places.

3. Columbia Harbour House in Liberty Square serves clam chowder and terrific Monte Cristo sandwiches.

4. Sleepy Hollow, also in Liberty Square, is good for chicken salad, Reuben sandwiches, Toll House cookies, and punch. The shady park across the street is a great place to relax while you snack.

5. If you feel like lighter fare, get a citrus swirl at the Sunshine Tree Terrace in Adventureland. Like Sleepy Hollow, this snack shop is tucked out of the way and has its own quiet courtyard.

The fast-food places in Fantasyland are a must to avoid. Likewise the Adventureland Veranda, where you wait far too long for mediocre Chinese food.

AFTERNOON RESTING PLACES

- The railroad
- The park across from Sleepy Hollow in Liberty Square
- The Diamond Horseshoe Jamboree
- The Hall of Presidents
- *Magic Journeys,* the 3-D film in Fantasyland
- Mission to Mars, the Carousel of Progress, the WEDway PeopleMover, and most Tomorrowland attractions
- Tom Sawyer Island
- *The Walt Disney Story* (film) on Main Street

BEST VANTAGE POINTS FOR WATCHING THE AFTERNOON AND EVENING PARADES

1. The absolutely best location is at the very beginning of Main Street, along the hub in front of the Railroad Station. (The parade begins here, emerging from behind City Hall.) The crowds grow less manageable as you proceed down Main Street and are at their worst in front of Cinderella Castle.

2. If you find yourself deep in the bowels of the theme park ½ hour before parade time, don't try to fight

your way up Main Street to the hub—you'll never make it. Instead, go to the end of the parade route, in front of Pecos Bill Cafe in Frontierland. The crowds here are much thinner than in front of Cinderella Castle or in Liberty Square.

BEST RESTROOM LOCATIONS IN THE MAGIC KINGDOM

1. Behind the Enchanted Grove snack bar near the Mad Tea Party.
2. In the passageway between Adventureland and Frontierland. This one is crowded but so huge that you never have to wait long.
3. If you're in the Baby Services center for other reasons, make a pit stop.
4. Most of the sit-down restaurants have their own restrooms, which are never very crowded.

THE MAGIC KINGDOM DON'T MISS LIST

- Space Mountain
- Pirates of the Caribbean
- Jungle Cruise
- Big Thunder Mountain Railroad
- Dumbo, the Flying Elephant
- It's a Small World
- Peter Pan's Flight
- Mickey's Starland (if your kids are preschoolers)
- The parades

THE MAGIC KINGDOM WORTH
YOUR WHILE LIST

- Swiss Family Treehouse
- Country Bear Vacation Hoedown
- Haunted Mansion
- Mad Tea Party
- The Hall of Presidents (if you have kids over 10)
- The rest of the Fantasyland rides (if your kids are preschoolers)

SPENDING YOUR LAST
HOUR IN THE PARK

1. During the on-season, when the Main Street Electrical Parade runs, take advantage of the fact that rides are empty at showtime. Lines at Space Mountain, Dumbo, the Flying Elephant, Jungle Cruise, and other popular attractions are more manageable just before closing.

2. If you opt to watch the parade, move up Main Street as far as possible to stake your curb space. Turn in your strollers before the parade starts, and be ready to make a fast exit once the last float rolls by.

3. Some rides—most notably Big Thunder Mountain Railroad, Cinderella's Golden Carrousel, and the skyway between Tomorrowland and Fantasyland—are particularly lovely at night.

THE SCARE FACTOR AT
THE MAGIC KINGDOM

Nothing at WDW is truly terrifying. In fact, young visitors raised on a steady diet of coasters called "Corkscrew" and "Python" are apt to find Disney offerings downright tame.

But Disney plays on your emotions in more subtle ways. Children who seem anesthetized by the violence in movies such as *Halloween VIII* have been known to sob inconsolably over the demise of Old Yeller. And the attention to detail that is so much a Disney trademark is especially evident in attractions like the new Great Movie Ride at MGM—when the alien lunges at you from above, he's believable.

Thus the scare factor is tough to gauge. With the exception of Space Mountain, nothing at WDW will knock off your glasses or shake out your fillings. But remember, Walt was the guy who bumped off Bambi's mother, and preschool children leave the attractions shaken in a totally different way.

The Rides

Snow White's Adventures

Don't expect to leave this attraction humming "Whistle While You Work." Riders take the role of Snow White as she flees through the woods, and the witch does leap out at you several times. But the ride is a short one, and the special effects are fairly simple.

Final verdict: Not too scary; fine for most kids over 4.

Mr. Toad's Wild Ride

Your car cereens through a fun house. At one point you "stall" on a railroad track with a train approaching.

Final verdict: Not scary at all.

Big Thunder Mountain Railroad

An exciting 3-minute ride, one of the best-loved in the MK. At no time does the train go very high, although it does travel fairly fast. Riders exit giggly but not shaky.

Final verdict: Fine for the 7 and over crowd. Children must be 40 inches tall to ride the train.

Haunted Mansion

More funny than scary. The teenagers who load you into black cars are dressed like morticians and never smile or meet your eyes . . . the ceiling in the portrait hall moves up . . . and the mansion is home to ravens, floating objects, swirling ghosts, glowing crystal balls, and doors that rap when there's no one there.

Final verdict: Fine for any child over 4 or 5.

Jungle Cruise

Your guide keeps things light with his running patter, and the elephants, rhinos, headshrinkers, and snakes are likewise played for laughs.

Final verdict: Fine for anyone.

Pirates of the Caribbean

My 4-year-old daughter grew a bit apprehensive as we wove our way through the drafty, dungeonlike queue area, but she loved the ride that followed. Although there are gunshots, skeletons, cannons, mangy-looking buccaneers, and even a brief drop over a "waterfall" in the dark, the mood is decidedly up.

Final verdict: Fine for anyone. In fact, over half the kids 7–11 surveyed listed Pirates as their favorite attraction at the MK.

Starjets

You can control how high your spaceship flies in this cyclic ride. A good choice for those not quite up to Space Mountain.

Final verdict: Fun for kids over 7 and preteens, although in terms of special effects the ride is no big deal.

Space Mountain

It's not just the fact that this is a roller coaster, it's that you plunge through utter darkness, which makes Space Mountain unique. There are lots of sharp dives with very little warning time. Kids under 7 must be with an adult, and children under 3 cannot ride.

Final verdict: Forget it for younger kids. Preteens and teenagers love it.

ON THE HORIZON: PLANS FOR THE MAGIC KINGDOM

Michael Eisner, chairman and CEO of the Walt Disney Company, has declared the 1990s "The Disney Decade." If you need any convincing, scan this list of planned attractions.

1. Coming in 1990: Two new stage shows, one titled The New Mickey Mouse Club, starring the talented kids seen daily on the Disney channel. The other show, Disney Afternoon, will feature the casts of Chip n' Dale's Rescue Rangers, Ducktales, and Talespin.

2. Coming in 1991: One Man's Dream, a salute to musical highlights of favorite Disney films such as *Peter Pan, Snow White,* and *The Jungle Book.*

3. Coming in 1992: A new CircleVision 360 adventure, combining Audio-Animatronics figures and film. The robots will "disappear" into the film, blending fantasy and reality.

4. Coming in 1993: Splash Mountain, based on that hot Disneyland attraction, will send visitors plunging down the side of a five-story mountain through Brer Rabbit's briar patch and into a misty pool below.

5. Coming in 1993: The Little Mermaid will carry young riders "under the sea."

6. Coming in 1996: A completely revamped Tomorrowland, designed as an intergalactic spaceport and featuring the Alien Encounter, a thrill ride that will pit "crew members" against the most terrifying alien in the universe. On a lighter note, the Galactic Revue will present an outer space musical starring a troupe of Audio-Animatronics jazz musicians. Remember the bar scene in *Star Wars?*

5

★ ★ ★ ★ ★ ★ ★ ★ ★ ★ ★ ★ ★ ★ ★ ★ ★ ★ ★

Epcot Center

EPCOT CENTER

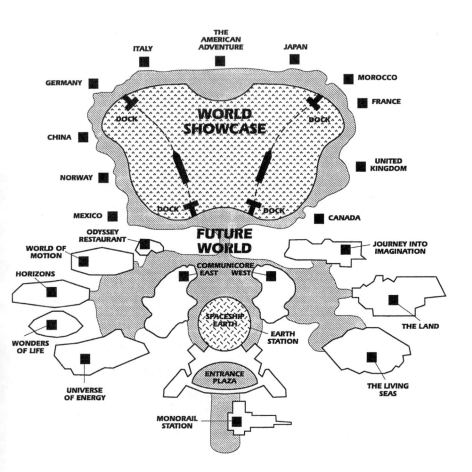

GETTING TO EPCOT CENTER

1. Epcot is easy to reach by car. If you arrive early in the morning, you can park very close to the main entrance gate and forgo the tram ride. If you arrive a bit later, however, the trams do run quickly and efficiently. Just be sure to write down your row number.

2. Many off-site hotels offer shuttle buses to Epcot. Fort Wilderness Campground Resort, The Disney Inn, and the Caribbean Beach Resort all offer their own shuttles as well.

3. If you're staying at the Polynesian Village Resort, Grand Floridian Resort, or Contemporary Resort, your fastest route is the monorail to the TTC; then transfer to the Epcot monorail.

4. The Walt Disney World Swan and Dolphin are connected to a special World Showcase entrance by canal. Take either the launch or shuttle bus.

GETTING AROUND EPCOT CENTER

As one of the players at the Comedy Warehouse on Pleasure Island suggests, Epcot stands for "every person comes out tired."

Epcot is indeed sprawling, but view the *FriendShip* launches that crisscross the World Showcase Lagoon and the double-decker buses as fun rides, not a serious means of transport. Your fastest means of getting around is walking.

SPENDING YOUR FIRST HOUR
IN EPCOT CENTER

1. As soon as you enter the main gate, veer left to rent strollers, and then, if it's operative, ride Spaceship Earth.

2. One parent should take the kids and the camera and order breakfast at the Stargate Restaurant (the Disney characters are often sighted here about 8:30 A.M.). The other parent should enter the WorldKey Information Services beneath Spaceship Earth, pick up an entertainment and special events schedule, and then make dining reservations.

3. After the ropes are dropped and you're allowed to enter the body of the park, make a beeline for the Wonders of Life pavilion. Ride Body Wars first.

EPCOT CENTER TOURING TIPS

1. Visit new attractions such as the Wonders of Life or the Norway pavilion first.

2. If you can't ride Spaceship Earth early in the morning, wait until evening.

3. Avoid the high-capacity shows such as Universe of Energy or *O Canada!* in the morning. Your time is better spent moving among the continuously loading attractions such as Body Wars, Horizons, The Land, World of Motion, The Living Seas, and Journey into Imagination. Save the theater-style attractions until the afternoon.

4. Touring Epcot is easier if you zig when everyone else zags. Future World stays crowded from midmorning until late afternoon and then empties as people head toward their dinner reservations in the World Showcase.

Avoid crowds by touring Future World until around noon and then drifting toward the World Showcase. Although no part of Epcot can truthfully be called empty in the afternoon, at least in the World Showcase you can escape to the films and indoor exhibits during the hottest and busiest times.

Then, perhaps after the 5 P.M. character show at the mouth of the World Showcase Lagoon, head back into Future World. Attractions such as Journey into Imagination and The Living Seas are rarely packed in the evenings.

5. If you're touring off-season and plan to spend mornings in the MK and evenings at Epcot, make your Epcot dinner reservations for as late as possible, leaving yourself several hours to tour before dinner.

6. Upon entering a World Showcase pavilion that has a film, such as France, Canada, America, or China, ask the attendant how long you have until the show begins. If the wait is 10 minutes or less, queue up. If the wait is longer, browse the pavilion shops until about 10 minutes until showtime. The World Showcase theaters are large, and everyone is almost always seated.

7. Most people circle the World Showcase Lagoon in a clockwise fashion, beginning with Mexico. You'll make better time if you move counterclockwise, beginning with Canada.

8. If you're not staying for IllumiNations, begin moving toward the main gates while the show is in progress.

FUTURE WORLD

Future World Attractions

Spaceship Earth

Few travelers, whatever their age, can remain blasé at the sight of Spaceship Earth, the most photographed and readily recognizable symbol of Epcot.

The ride inside, which coils toward the top of the 17-story geosphere, traces developments in communication from cave drawings to computers. The voice of Walter Cronkite booms in your ear as you climb past scenes of Egyptian temples, the Gutenberg press, and a performance of *Oedipus Rex*. Even preschoolers rated Spaceship Earth highly, probably due to the excitement of actually entering the "big ball" and the impressive finale, which flashes a planetarium sky above you as you swirl backward down through the darkness.

The Living Seas

This relatively new attraction, featuring a saltwater aquarium so enormous that Spaceship Earth could float inside it, is one of the most popular at Epcot with kids 7–11. You begin with a short film that discusses the critical role of the ocean as a source of energy and then swiftly move on to board gondolas which take you through an underwater viewing tunnel. More than 200 varieties of marine life, including stingrays, dolphins, barracuda, sharks, and an occasional scuba-clad Mickey, swim above you.

The most enjoyable part of the attraction, however, comes after you disembark at Sea Base Alpha. You can remain here as long as you choose, wandering through two levels of observation tanks that allow you to view the fishes and the human divers at startlingly close quarters. (Interested kids sometimes get a chance to suit up in diving gear, but don't worry—despite teasing, the Disney cast has no intention of letting visitors into the tank.)

Note: It's easy to spend an entire afternoon at The Living Seas. But if you plan to devote a day to Sea World while in Orlando, you'll find much of the same stuff there, so hold your time at The Living Seas to a minimum.

The Land

This cheerful pavilion is home to three separate attractions as well as a rotating restaurant and fast-food court. Because it's the hub of so much activity, The Land is crowded from midmorning on. If you can't visit it before 11 A.M., wait until evening.

Listen to the Land   The theme here is food and how we get it. Visitors travel by boat past scenes of various farming environments, ending with a peek at fish farming, drip irrigation, and other innovative agricultural technologies. Perhaps because there are few special effects and no cute "tourguide" such as Figment, who lives in the Journey into Imagination pavilion next door, this attraction is less interesting to preschoolers. But, as is the case with all Future World attractions, the ride moves swiftly, and the educational aspects are winningly presented. In short, this won't be a child's favorite attraction, but she won't complain either.

Symbiosis   This film, which graphically illustrates how easily people can ruin their own environment, is timely and terrific for adults and kids over 12. Younger kids will be bored senseless, which isn't all bad—more than one youngster has napped during the presentation.

Kitchen Kabaret   An Audio-Animatronics show about nutrition, the Kabaret has been largely overlooked by reviewers. Hostess Bonnie Appetit and a crop of singing vegetables are only slightly less appealing than the Country Bear Vacation Hoedown in the MK. And a chance to sit for 20 minutes in a cool, dark, rarely crowded theater is pretty appealing as well.

Journey into Imagination

This is one of the best pavilions in Future World for young kids. The ride inside features Dreamfinder and the charming purple Figment of his imagination. Together they take you through a variety of scenes celebrating art, literature, music, and other products of human creativity. Be forewarned—there's a sudden flash of light near the end of the ride. This pavilion is sponsored by Kodak, and a wide-screen photograph of you in all your glory is waiting around the next turn.

After that horrible sight, nothing in the 3-D film *Captain EO* will scare you. When *EO* debuted, some adults were put off by the idea of an 18-minute rock video, but *Captain EO,* which stars Michael Jackson, is state of the art and surprisingly funny. This attraction received the highest rating of any in Epcot Center by kids 10–14 and praise from every age group. Several families reported that their kids insisted on seeing the movie more than once.

After you disembark from Journey into Imagination, a huge digital clock tells you how many minutes until the next presentation of *Captain EO*. While you wait, it's fun to explore the Image Works, a series of hands-on exhibits such as the Magic Palette, with an electronic paintbrush, or Stepping Tones, where kids can create music by jumping into differently colored puddles of light. If it sounds bizarre, it's because it is, but modern children catch on swiftly and may deign to explain to their parents how the exhibits work.

World of Motion

It's Fun to Be Free, the ride enclosed in the General Motors World of Motion exhibit, is described as "an Audio-Animatronics survey of the history of transportation," a description that does nothing to convey the sheer joy of the ride. The robots here are the most humorous and lifelike in Future World—check out the exasperated expression on the Mona Lisa's face as Leonardo deserts her to conduct a flight experiment or the astonishment of the rider whose stagecoach is under Indian attack. Best of all, there's rarely much of a wait at this fast-loading attraction. The TransCenter at the end of the line appeals to youngsters with motor fetishes but contains mostly passive exhibits, with far fewer opportunities for active play than Journey into Imagination or Wonders of Life.

Horizons

How will the average family live in the future? General Electric takes riders into the next century, where robots clean house, families "visit" via holographic telephone, and cities flourish on the ocean floor. Needless to say, Disney's predictions for the year 2020 are all sunny, and children love the final special effect, which allows them to press a button and choose whether their journey will end in space, on land, or undersea.

Horizons, like World of Motion, loads fast and is rarely too crowded. These two pavilions are good choices when the new Wonders of Life next door is swamped.

Wonders of Life

Devoted to celebrating the human body, the Wonders of

Life pavilion resembles a brightly colored street fair full of hands-on exhibits. You can check out your health profile via computer, get advice on your tennis or golf swing, and test your endurance on a motorized bike. Kids enjoy the film *Goofy About Health* and the Sensory Funhouse. (Despite the provocative name, this exhibit is devoted to only the most wholesome of tactile sensations.) Like The Land, the Wonders pavilion houses three major attractions and a food court; it's crowded by 11 A.M. Until the novelty of this new pavilion subsides, early morning touring is strongly advised.

Body Wars   As close as Epcot Center comes to a pure thrill ride, Body Wars incorporates the same flight-simulation technology found at MGM's Star Tours to take riders on a turbulent high-speed thrill ride through the human body. After being miniaturized to the size of a pinhead and injected into a patient, the crew is briefed to expect a routine medical mission for the purpose of removing a splinter from the "safe zone just under the skin." But when shapely Dr. Lair is sucked into a capillary, your crew is off on a rescue chase through the heart, lungs, and brain.

No expectant mothers or kids under 3 are allowed to board, but others shouldn't be frightened by all the posted warnings. The occasional Body Wars queasy-making moments are due more to the accuracy of flight-simulation technology than to the bouncing of the spaceship.

Note: If you're traveling with a child under 3, attendants will help you split up the family so that everyone else can still ride. If dad and the older kids go on one flight, for example, mom and the baby can wait in the holding dock. After dad disembarks, mom can hand over the baby and ride herself.

The Making of Me   This film is a fetus-eye view of conception, gestation, and birth. Lyrical and sensitive, it's appropriate for any age.

Cranium Command   *Cranium Command* is a hilarious film and Audio-Animatronics show, by far the funniest presentation in Epcot Center. General Knowledge taps an unfortunate recruit, Buzzy, to pilot "the most unstable craft in the fleet," the brain of a 12-year-old boy. If he fails in his mission, Buzzy will be demoted to flying the brain of a chicken or, worse, a talk show host. Buzzy tries to guide his boy through a typical day of junior high school without overloading his system, which isn't easy, especially when the body parts are played by this cast: Charles Grodin as the right brain, Jon Lovitz as the left brain, Hans and Franz from "Saturday Night Live" pumping it up in the role of the heart, Norm from "Cheers" as the stomach, and, in a particularly convincing performance, Bobcat Goldthwait as adrenaline.

Universe of Energy

People of all ages can enjoy this technologically complex presentation. Kids are dazzled by the dinosaurs, and parents leave the pavilion muttering "How did they do that?"

Children under 12 may be bored by the opening film, which examines worldwide energy sources. But you soon file into a conventional-looking theater for a second, shorter film about the development of fossil fuels during the prehistoric era. Then comes the Disney twist: The 97-seat theater begins to break apart in sections that align themselves in sequence and move toward the screen. Your theater has become your train, and the screen slowly lifts to reveal an Audio-Animatronics version of the film you've just viewed. The air reeks of sulfur, as it presumably did during the prehistoric era, the light is eerily blue, and all around you are those darn dinosaurs, the largest Disney robots ever created and unnervingly authentic. The ride concludes with a final film on the future of energy in a separate auditorium, after your train has once again metamorphosed into a theater. Most amazingly of all, you learn that your moving train has been entirely fueled by the solar panels on top of the Universe of Energy pavilion.

Note: Some kids are frightened by the dinosaurs. Also, the Universe of Energy seats a large number of people at a time, meaning that lines form and dissipate quickly. If the line looks prohibitive, check out nearby pavilions and return in ½ hour; you may be able to walk right in.

Future World is also the home of CommuniCore East and CommuniCore West, two crescent-shaped plazas full of shops, restaurants, and technological exhibits. The attractions look intimidating, but most kids get the hang of them quickly and enjoy playing with the computers, touch-sensitive TV screens, and robots. Although you probably won't have time for the CommuniCores if you're trying to tour Epcot in 1 day, visitors with more time are often surprised by how much they enjoy spending an hour here. Teens and preteens rated Expo Robotics, an exhibit where a robot actually draws your picture, highest of all CommuniCore exhibits.

WORLD SHOWCASE

World Showcase Attractions

O Canada!
This 20-minute CircleVision 360 film is gorgeous, stir-

ring—and nearly impossible to view with young kids. To be able to enjoy the effect of the circular screen, guests are required to stand during the presentation, and strollers aren't allowed into the theater, which means that babies and toddlers must be held and preschoolers, who can't see anything in a room full of standing adults, often clamor to be lifted up as well. It's a backbreaking experience.

So we regretfully suggest that families with kids under 7 pass up this presentation, as well as the equally lovely *Wonders of China: Land of Beauty, Land of Time*. Possible solution: Canada and China are both located near the World Showcase Plaza, where the afternoon character show is held. If one adult volunteers to stay with the kids during the show, the other will have ample time to slip back to China or Canada and view one of the films. Another possibility: If you're dining at one of the Epcot Center restaurants, your parents' night out is also a good time to see the World Showcase films.

Impressions de France

What a difference a seat makes. Like all the Epcot films, *Impressions* is exceedingly well done, with lush music and a 200-degree wide-screen feel. It's fairly easy to get in, even in the afternoon, and no one minds if babies take a little nap.

The American Adventure

This multimedia presentation, combining Audio-Animatronics figures with film, is very popular with all age groups. (Surprisingly, teenagers rated this highly patriotic show as their second favorite Epcot attraction, just behind *Captain EO*.) The technological highlight of the show is when the Ben Franklin robot actually walks upstairs to visit Thomas Jefferson, but the 30-minute presentation is full of elaborate sets that rise from the stage, film montages, and painless history lessons.

Note: The pavilion becomes quite crowded in the afternoon, but since it's located at the exact midpoint of the World Showcase lagoon, it's impractical to skip it and work your way back later. If faced with a ½-hour wait, enjoy the excellent Voices of Liberty preshow, or grab a snack at the Liberty Inn next door.

Wonders of China: Land of Beauty, Land of Time

See the *O Canada!* section.

Maelstrom

Along with The American Adventure, the Norway pavilion features a boat ride that's the favorite World Showcase attraction of kids under 12. Your Viking ship sails through fjords and storms, over waterfalls, past a threatening three-headed troll—all within a breathtaking 4 minutes. Riders disembark in a North Sea coastal village, where a short film is presented. The Norway pavilion is the newest of the World Showcase nations and draws large crowds all day. Take Maelstrom early in the morning if possible, or just before the park closing, when most people have lined up to await IllumiNations.

El Rio del Tiempo: The River of Time

There's rarely a wait for this charming boat ride, located inside the romantic Mexico pavilion. Reminiscent of It's a Small World in the MK, El Rio is especially appealing to younger riders.

GENERAL INFORMATION ON EPCOT CENTER RESTAURANTS

1. Among the families we surveyed, there was a great difference of opinion as to which Epcot Center restau-

rants are best. "We loved Alfredo's," writes one family, "but the Coral Reef was a big disappointment. It was overpriced, and you can get the same view for free upstairs at The Living Seas." "The Coral Reef was our absolute favorite," writes another family. "Alfredo's, on the other hand, is a waste of time." (L'Originale Alfredo di Roma Ristorante and the Coral Reef Restaurant are the most expensive, most popular—and most controversial—Epcot eateries. Perhaps because reservations are so hard to come by, diners enter with exalted expectations and leave either profoundly disappointed or convinced that they've had a mountaintop experience.)

2. If you're staying on-site, you can make reservations for both dinner and lunch up to 2 days in advance by dialing 824-4000. Such foresight may be necessary if you're aiming to get into the Coral Reef on a Friday night in July.

If you aren't staying on-site, make your reservations first thing in the morning at Worldkey Information Services under Spaceship Earth. Visitors without reservations sometimes get seated by simply showing up at the restaurant door, especially if they try a large restaurant like the Biergarten or eat dinner very early.

3. If you'd like to try several Epcot restaurants, remember that lunchtime selections are just as impressive as those at dinner, and the fare is much cheaper then.

4. Kids are welcome at any Epcot eatery, although some are more entertaining for youngsters than others. High chairs, booster seats, and kiddie menus are universally available.

5. Casual attire is OK anywhere in the park. It may seem strange to eat oysters with champagne sauce while wearing a Goofy sweatshirt, but you'll get used to it.

6. The Epcot restaurants take their reservations seriously. If you show up at the Mitsukoshi Restaurant at 12:45 for a 12:30 reservation, expect to be told "sayonara."

7. Be careful when booking for France, which is home to two sit-down restaurants: Chefs de France, which is streetfront, and Bistro de Paris upstairs. Many visitors get these places confused and risk losing their reservation by showing up at the wrong place.

8. Be bold. Your hometown probably has good Chinese and Italian restaurants, but how often do you get to sample Norwegian or Moroccan food?

9. Epcot dining isn't cheap. Dinner for a family of four at a restaurant described in the following section as "moderately priced" will still run about $50 without drinks or wine.

FULL-SERVICE RESTAURANTS IN EPCOT CENTER

How much is this place going to cost? Is the service so slow we'll miss IllumiNations? Is it hard to get reservations? Is there anything to keep the kids entertained while the adults sip their sake? Read on for an overview of the suitability of the full-service restaurants for kids. (The Dining Without the Kids part of Section 8—Disney World After Dark—more fully describes most of these eating establishments.)

Chefs de France (France)
   Cost: Moderate to high, but worth it.
   Booking: Difficult.

Suitability for kids: Moderate. It's fun to watch the crowds go by, but the tables are close and the waiters move at quite a clip, so there's no place for children to stand and stretch their legs.

Bistro de Paris (France)
Cost: Moderate to high, but worth it.

Booking: Difficult.

Suitability for kids: Low. This is one of the more romantic Epcot Center restaurants, with dim lighting and leisurely service. Try it on the night you leave the kids back at the Mouseketeer Club.

Rose & Crown Pub & Dining Room (United Kingdom)
Cost: Moderate.

Booking: Easy.

Suitability for kids: High, especially if you eat outside and can watch the *FriendShip* launches go by on the lagoon.

Comments: A nice pub atmosphere with charming service but mediocre food.

Mitsukoshi Restaurant (Japan)
Cost: Moderate to high, and overpriced.

Booking: Easy.

Suitability for kids: High.

Comments: Diners sit at large common tables while chefs slice and dice flamboyantly. If there's a Benihana in your hometown, you get the idea.

L'Originale Alfredo di Roma Ristorante (Italy)
Cost: High, and generally considered overpriced.

Booking: Very difficult.

Suitability for kids: Moderate. Most children like Italian food, and the kiddie menu is well conceived, but the restaurant is very crowded.

Comments: Despite the elegant surroundings, this isn't a good location for romantic dining. Try it at lunch.

Marrakesh (Morocco)
Cost: Moderate.

Booking: Easy.

Suitability for kids: High. The surroundings, with lots of elbow room, are exotic, and kids enjoy the belly dancers.

Nine Dragons Restaurant (China)
Cost: High, and overpriced.

Booking: Easy.

Suitability for kids: Moderate.

Comments: Nothing special.

San Angel Inn Restaurante (Mexico)
Cost: Moderate.

Booking: It's fairly difficult to get reservations here, especially at lunch.

Suitability for kids: High. The service is swift and friendly, and kids can browse among the market stalls of the Mexico pavilion while waiting for the food.

Comments: One of the best bets in Epcot Center. San Angel didn't receive a single unfavorable review.

Biergarten (Germany)
Cost: Moderate.

Booking: Easy.

Suitability for kids: High. There's plenty of room to move about, a rousing, noisy atmosphere, and entertainment in the form of yodelers and an oompah-pah band.

Akershus (Norway)
Cost: Moderate.

Booking: Moderate.

Suitability for kids: High. There's a buffet, so you can get your food immediately, and picky eaters get a chance to select from a huge variety of foods.

Comments: A fine spot for hearty eaters since you can load up at the hot and cold buffet tables. This is also a good chance to sample a variety of unusual dishes. Although diners were a bit nervous about the Akershus when it first opened, it's growing more popular, and harder to book, each month.

The Land Grille Room (The Land pavilion)
Cost: Moderate.

Booking: Tough to book at lunch, easy at dinner.

Suitability for kids: High. Easily recognizable American dishes, large booths that let you stretch out, and the restaurant rotates, allowing diners to observe scenes from the Listen to the Land boat ride below.

Comments: The only full-service restaurant in Epcot that offers breakfast. The crepes are outstanding.

Coral Reef Restaurant (The Living Seas pavilion)
Cost: High—the most expensive restaurant in Epcot.

Booking: Extremely difficult.

Suitability for kids: Moderate. It's fun to watch the fish, but the children's menu is pricey.

Comments: If you want to sample fresh seafood while in Florida, the innumerable restaurants in Orlando are cheaper and easier to get into.

DECENT FAST-FOOD RESTAURANTS IN EPCOT CENTER

Fast food is a somewhat relative term at Epcot, where long lines are the norm during peak dining hours. But the choices are far more varied and interesting than those at the MK. In the World Showcase, try:

1. The Yakitori House in the Japan pavilion features delicious skewered chicken.

2. Cantina de San Angel in the Mexico pavilion is noted for their tortillas and tostadas.

3. Kringla Bakeri og Kafe in the Norway pavilion has open-faced salmon or ham sandwiches and unusual pastries.

4. Le Cellier in Canada, Epcot's only cafeteria, has wonderful pork and potato pie. Blood sugar a bit low from all the walking? A slab of maple syrup pie will pick you up fast.

5. The Liberty Inn at the American pavilion is great if your kids are suffering hamburger withdrawal, and the Odyssey Restaurant offers indoor dining and fairly fast counter service.

6. The Farmer's Market in The Land pavilion is a good choice if you find yourself in Future World at lunchtime or your party can't agree on a restaurant. The food court here features plenty of choices, including clam chowder, quiche, barbecue, stuffed potatoes, scooped-out pineapples filled with fruit salad, and killer chocolate chip cookies.

EPCOT CENTER EXTRAS

1. *Character sightings*

- Visit with the gang around 8:30 or 9 A.M. in the Stargate Restaurant.
- Often the characters visit World Showcase nations between 2 P.M. and 4 P.M. Pluto wears a serape, Minnie a cancan ensemble, Daisy Duck a kimono, Goofy bagpipes and a kilt; Mickey is decked out as a Canadian Mountie.
- Twenty or more characters arrive at the mouth of the World Showcase Lagoon by double-decker bus around 5 P.M. daily for a loud, cheerful musical extravaganza and 20-minute autograph-signing session afterward. Check your entertainment schedule for exact showtimes.

2. *Special shows:* Singers, dancers, jugglers, and artisans from around the globe perform throughout the World Showcase daily. Most of these presentations (which are detailed in your daily entertainment guide) are not especially oriented toward children, although kids over 7 will catch the humor of the Renaissance Street Players in the United Kingdom or the Teatro di Bologna in Italy.

Sometimes very special performers, such as Chinese acrobats or stars of the Moscow circus, are showcased in Future World. These acts draw high ratings from kids in every age group.

3. *IllumiNations:* This display of laser technology, fireworks, syncopated fountains, and classical music is a real-life Fantasia and well on its way to becoming a WDW classic. Very popular, very crowded, and a perfect way to end an Epcot day, IllumiNations takes place on the World Showcase Lagoon, and the performance coincides with the park closing time. Try to watch from the

Mexico or Canada pavilion so you'll be able to beat most of the crowd to the exits afterward. (If you're staying at the Swan or Dolphin and leaving via the "back door" exit, try the America pavilion for an unobstructed view and plenty of seating.)

BEST RESTROOM LOCATIONS IN EPCOT CENTER

The restrooms within the Future World pavilions are always crowded, and those within the CommuniCores aren't much better. But there are places where you can take a relatively quick potty break:

- The Odyssey Restaurant. (Baby Services is also located here, so you can take care of everyone's needs with one stop.)
- The restroom between the Germany and Italy pavilions.
- The restroom between the Morocco and France pavilions.
- The restroom near the Group Sales Booth in the Entrance Plaza (near the monorail, and a good place to stop as you exit the park).
- Most of the sit-down restaurants have their own restrooms.

AFTERNOON RESTING PLACES

- Universe of Energy.
- *Symbiosis* in The Land pavilion.
- The American Adventure.
- *Impressions de France.*

- Electronic Forum in CommuniCore East. (The Future Choice Theater represents Epcot's ongoing survey of public opinion. Participants answer polling questions by pushing a button. Results are immediately flashed onscreen and later distributed to *USA Today* and other publications—a fun way to kill an hour.)

EPCOT CENTER DON'T MISS LIST

- Spaceship Earth
- Body Wars in the Wonders of Life pavilion
- *Cranium Command* in the Wonders of Life pavilion
- Universe of Energy
- It's Fun to Be Free in the World of Motion pavilion
- *Captain EO* in the Journey into Imagination pavilion
- Journey into Imagination
- The Living Seas (If you're not touring Sea World later in the week)
- The American Adventure in the American pavilion
- Maelstrom ride in the Norway pavilion
- *Impressions de France* in the France pavilion
- IllumiNations

EPCOT CENTER WORTH YOUR WHILE LIST

- *The Making of Me* in the Wonders of Life pavilion
- Listen to the Land in The Land pavilion
- Kitchen Kabaret in The Land pavilion

- Horizons
- CommuniCore West and East
- Image Works in the Journey into Imagination pavilion
- El Rio del Tiempo: The River of Time in the Mexico pavilion
- *Wonders of China: Land of Beauty, Land of Time* in the China pavilion
- *O Canada!* in the Canada pavilion
- The 5 P.M. Disney character show

THE SCARE FACTOR AT EPCOT CENTER

The Rides

The Maelstrom in Norway
This new ride sounds terrifying—you encounter three-headed trolls, become caught in a North Sea storm, and narrowly miss going over a waterfall backward. The reality is a very tame but charming ride. Kids seem especially enchanted by the fact that you ride in Viking ships, and the much-touted "backward plunge over a waterfall" is so subtle that passengers in the front of the boat aren't even aware of the impending danger.
     Final verdict: Fine for all.

Journey into Imagination
Surprisingly, many preschool children report that they're frightened by the googly eyed purple Figment. This attraction, while one of the more child-oriented in Future World, does have a dark segment that explores the world of mystery.

Final verdict: Most kids adore Figment, but if your child is a bit put off, one parent could always wait with the youngster in Image Works while the rest of the family rides.

Universe of Energy

Again, preschoolers have a range of reactions. The dinosaurs are extremely real looking, and some of them bend fairly low over your passing theater car, dripping vines from their mouths. Most kids are such dinosaur junkies that they scream only when it's time to get off, but some children are genuinely frightened.

Final verdict: Probably fine for everyone, unless you have a very young child who has trouble distinguishing reality from illusion.

Body Wars in the Wonders of Life

The Disney PR people must love the word "plunge," for this ride too is described as "plunging through the human immune system as you dodge blood cells and antibodies at breakneck speed in a race against attacking organisms that threaten to destroy your craft and you!" Makes you breathless just to read it, huh?

The ride is indeed thrilling, but most of these effects are visual. You don't actually plunge, but you feel as if you do.

Final verdict: The whole family will appreciate this one, albeit on different levels. The other attractions in Wonders of Life, such as the clever *Cranium Command,* which explores life through the brain of a 12-year-old boy, are equally appropriate for any age, and the film on childbirth (*The Making of Me*) is realistic without being too overwhelming for young viewers.

ON THE HORIZON: PLANS
FOR EPCOT CENTER

Expect two new countries in the World Showcase and two new teen-oriented attractions in Future World.

1. Coming in 1994: A new 3-D video from George Lucas, promised to be even more dazzling than *Captain EO*.
2. Coming in 1994: The Soviet Union pavilion.
3. Also in 1994: The Switzerland pavilion, featuring The Matterhorn Bobsled Ride.
4. Coming in 1995: A new Future World pavilion, Journeys in Space, which will use flight-simulation technology to reproduce the look and feel of an outer-space experience.

6

★ ★ ★ ★ ★ ★ ★ ★ ★ ★ ★ ★ ★ ★ ★ ★ ★

Disney-MGM
Studios
Theme Park

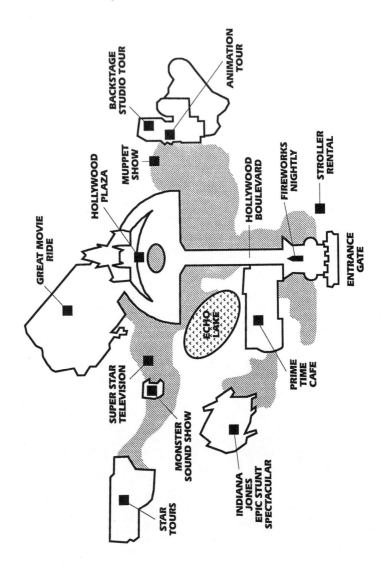

DISNEY-MGM STUDIOS

BACKSTAGE STUDIO TOUR

ANIMATION TOUR

HOLLYWOOD PLAZA

MUPPET SHOW

GREAT MOVIE RIDE

HOLLYWOOD BOULEVARD

FIREWORKS NIGHTLY

STROLLER RENTAL

ENTRANCE GATE

ECHO LAKE

SUPER STAR TELEVISION

MONSTER SOUND SHOW

PRIME TIME CAFE

INDIANA JONES EPIC STUNT SPECTACULAR

STAR TOURS

GETTING TO DISNEY-MGM STUDIOS THEME PARK

Compared to the MK, getting through the MGM gates is a snap.

1. Shuttle buses run approximately every 15 minutes from the TTC, Epcot, and all on-site hotels.
2. If you're staying off-site and have a car, note that the MGM parking lot is small. Many guests forgo the parking lot tram and walk to the front gate.

SPENDING YOUR FIRST HOUR AT DISNEY-MGM STUDIOS THEME PARK

1. Once you're through the gate, one parent can handle stroller rental at Oscar's Classic Car Souvenirs & Super Service Station while the other picks up an entertainment schedule at Guest Relations. *Note:* Unlike the strollers at Epcot and the MK, MGM strollers are the lightweight "sling" kind and easy to load onto the Backstage Studio Tour tram.
2. Move down Hollywood Boulevard quickly; there'll be time to shop in midafternoon or evening. If you haven't had breakfast, check out the pastries at Starring Rolls.
3. Board the Great Movie Ride.
4. Board Star Tours.
5. Make reservations at the 50's Prime Time Cafe or the Hollywood Brown Derby if you're interested in a sit-down lunch or dinner.
6. Head for the Backstage Studio Tour. You should try to do the Great Movie Ride, Star Tours, and the Backstage Studio Tour before lunch.

MGM TOURING TIPS

1. Save theater-style presentations such as Super-Star Television, the Indiana Jones Epic Stunt Spectacular, and the Monster Sound Show for afternoon or evening. Tour continuous-loading attractions such as the Great Movie Ride and Star Tours early in the day.

2. The Disney people have posted a gigantic blackboard at the end of Hollywood Boulevard, to keep visitors updated on approximate waiting times at various attractions. Consult it whenever you're in doubt about what to do next.

3. Your entertainment schedule not only provides showtimes but also gives you information on the Celebrity of the Day and what shows are filming. If the "All New Mickey Mouse Club," "Win, Lose, or Draw," "Let's Make a Deal," or any other Disney channel shows are in production on the day of your visit, Guest Relations can tell you how to become a member of the studio audience.

4. MGM is small and easily crisscrossed, so don't feel obligated to tour attractions in any particular geographic sequence. Those 4- and 5-year olds who would need a stroller at the MK or Epcot can do without one here.

5. If you miss an attraction like the popular Indiana Jones Epic Stunt Spectacular show in the afternoon, return in the evening. It's also easier to get tapped for SuperStar Television at one of the less-crowded evening shows.

6. The closing fireworks display, while nothing compared to IllumiNations, is still a fun way to end the day.

MGM Attractions

The Great Movie Ride

Housed in the Chinese Theater at the end of Hollywood Boulevard, The Great Movie Ride debuted as an instant classic. Disney's largest ride-through attraction, it loads steadily and fairly swiftly, but The Great Movie Ride draws large crowds and is best toured either early in the morning or in the last hour before the park closes.

Each tram holds approximately 30 riders, and your tour guide provides an amusing spiel as you glide past soundstage sets from *Casablanca, Aliens, The Wizard of Oz,* and other great films. The Audio-Animatronics figures of Gene Kelly, Julie Andrews, and Clint Eastwood are among Disney's best.

Things suddenly turn ugly as your car stalls and the movie scenes come to life. Depending on which car you've boarded, you're about to be overrun by either a gangster on the lam from James Cagney or a desperado trying to escape John Wayne. Your tour guide may be gunned down or your tram taken hostage, but don't fret too much. In the last scene, drawn from *Indiana Jones and the Temple of Doom,* expect another stunning twist of fortune, just in time to reestablish justice and guarantee a happy ending.

Star Tours

Motion-simulation technology and a slightly jostling cabin combine to produce the real feel of flight in Star Tours, the MGM version of the highly acclaimed Disneyland ride. With the hapless Captain Rex at the helm, your crew is off for what is promised as a routine mission to the Moon of Endor. But if you think this mission is going to be routine, you don't know diddly about Disney. "Don't worry if this is your first flight," Rex comforts visitors as they board. "It's my first one too." One wrong turn later and you're ripping through the fabric of space at hyperspeed, headed toward combat with the dreaded Death Star.

George Lucas served as creative consultant, and the ride echoes the charming as well as the terrifying elements of his *Star Wars* series. The chatter of R2D2, C3PO, and assorted droids make even the queues enjoyable, and when you finally land you're in the village of Ewoks. Star Tours is the best of both worlds, with visual effects so convincing that you'll clutch your armrails, but its actual rumbles so mild that only the youngest children are eliminated as potential crew members. If the teenagers scarfing up silver satin jackets and other memorabilia at the adjacent Endor Vendors gift shop are any indication, Star Tours will be the hot Disney ride for 1991.

Ride Star Tours immediately upon entering the park.

Note: As in Body Wars at Epcot, Disney attendants are happy to help families traveling with children under 3 break up their party so that everyone except the baby gets to ride.

SuperStar Television

Want to belly up to the bar at "Cheers"? Ride the range with the Cartwrights? Be discovered by Ed Sullivan or chat with Carson? You get your chance at the highly inventive SuperStar Television, where special effects integrate the actions of audience volunteers with footage from well-known TV shows.

To volunteer as an actor, show up at the preshow holding area about 20 minutes before the stated performance time. (Showtimes for SuperStar Television, the Monster Sound Show, and the Indiana Jones Epic Stunt Spectacular vary from day to day, so consult your trusty entertainment schedule.) If your kids would like to join the cast of "Gilligan's Island" or be interviewed by Howard Cosell, there's no secret to getting selected: Work your way to the front of the crowd and shamelessly wave your arms—they aren't looking for shy people here. In fact, kids tapped to perform remembered SuperStar Television as the highlight of their MGM day. If you aren't chosen in one casting section, you can always exit the holding area without seeing the show and try again later.

Once you're selected, you'll be taken backstage for costuming and a brief rehersal while the rest of the gang files into the 1,000-seat theater. Most volunteers respond ably, and the results are usually quite funny. Because of the large seating area, SuperStar Television is a good choice for midafternoon, but if you don't catch it then, try the evening shows, which are never crowded.

Monster Sound Show

This theater is the smallest at MGM, so check the size of the line before you queue up to watch a funny movie featuring Chevy Chase and Martin Short. Audience volunteers add sound effects to the short film; when the tape is rolled back, the mistakes are screechingly funny. Most kids love this show, and the SoundWorks exhibits as you exit are also a good way to kill a ½ hour. (Especially neat are the Phonic Funnies, which let you dub your own voice onto films starring Snow White or Roger Rabbit.) The Monster Sound Show is generally a fine choice for afternoon.

Animation Building Tour

Don't be put off by the name. This 40-minute tour is fast-paced, and the preshow featuring Walter Cronkite and Robin Williams is hilarious.

Like the Backstage Studio Tour next door, the tour after the show is divided into two parts. The walking tour gives you a chance to see Disney animators at work; the tour winds up with a theater production featuring animated Disney classics, which greatly appeals to preschool age kids.

This is a good choice for evening. The touring groups are relatively small, so it's tough to get in in the afternoon.

Indiana Jones Epic Stunt Spectacular

Next to Star Tours, this is teens' and preteens' favorite MGM attraction. You may think the lines are the most spectacular part of the show, but because the 2,000-seat theater is so huge, people standing as far back as the 50's Prime Time Cafe are usually seated. Line up about 20 minutes before showtime, and be aware that afternoon shows are often a mob scene. If they are, try again during one of the last two seatings of the evening.

As in the other theater presentations, audience volunteers are chosen. (Your odds of being tapped improve if you're sitting near center front.) Professional stunt people re-create daring scenes from the Indiana Jones series, and it's a great chance to learn how those difficult and dangerous stunts end up on film.

Backstage Studio Tour

This is a major attraction; the tour takes about 2 hours to complete. Your best time to begin is midmorning, after riding Star Tours and The Great Movie Ride. If you can't make it before lunch, wait until late afternoon.

The tour begins with a tram ride that scoots you through wardrobe and prop departments and then past huge outdoor sets representing a typical small town and a large city. You'll see the exterior of the home where the Golden Girls "live." The highlight of the tram segment is a stop in Catastrophe Canyon, where you'll be caught in a flash flood, an oil explosion, and an earthquake. (The flood is most convincing; prepare to get wet.) Later you'll ride behind the canyon and see how the disasters were created.

After you disembark from your tram, pause for a restroom break, a snack, or taking pictures among the Roger Rabbit props. You can begin the walking segment of the tour at leisure.

Kids enjoy this part most. You can see a naval battle and a storm at sea created in the special effects water tank and view real soundstages where Disney shows such as the "All New Mickey Mouse Club" may be in production. Two kids from the audience are chosen to reproduce the infamous flying bee scene from *Honey, I Shrunk the Kids*. Next you'll watch Bette Midler in a clever 4-minute film called *The Lottery* and then walk through the soundstage where the film was made, checking out the props and special effects equipment up close. Finally, in the postproduction segment of the walking tour, you'll sit back in a theater and enjoy previews of new Disney/Touchstone releases.

The Backstage Studio Tour is a big deal, and you'll probably want to stop for a meal and a rest afterward. But Disney does a good job of mixing in humor with the more technical information as well as using big-name stars, from Warren Beatty to Pee Wee Herman, as "teachers," so most kids hold up with the tour better than you might expect.

Coming Soon: The Muppet Show

Jim Henson served as creative consultant for the Muppet pavilion, which is slated to open in late 1990 and is the only MGM attraction specifically directed to young children. Expect a musical stage show titled Here Come the Muppets and a Muppet All-Star Parade presented daily along Hollywood Boulevard. By 1991, a Muppet 3-D film and a large-scale attraction, The Muppet Movie Ride, will be in place.

FULL-SERVICE RESTAURANTS AND CAFETERIA AT MGM

Although, like the rest of WDW, MGM is hardly a bastion of haute cuisine, the food here is fun. Reservations are taken at the door of the 50's Prime Time Cafe and the Hollywood Brown Derby and should be made fairly soon after you enter the park.

1. *50's Prime Time Cafe*
The 50's Prime Time Cafe, with its kitsch decor and ditsy waitresses dressed like June Cleaver, is almost an attraction in itself. Meatloaf, macaroni, milkshakes, and other comfort food are served in a 50s-style kitchen while dozens of TVs blare clips from classic sitcoms in the background.

"Hi, kids," says your waitress, pulling up a chair to the formica-topped table. "You didn't leave your bikes in the driveway, did you? Let me see those hands." Assuming that you pass her clean fingernails inspection, "mom" will go on to advise you on your food choices. "I'll bring peas with that. Vegetables are good for you."

The camp is lost on young kids, who nonetheless love the no-frills food and the fact that mom brings around crayons and coloring books and then hangs their artwork with magnets on the front of a refrigerator. But it's baby boomer parents, raised on the sitcoms the restaurant spoofs, who really adore the place. The tacky Tune In Lounge next door is decorated in exact replicas of the furniture my parents had in their den 35 years ago. Much of MGM is dedicated to nostalgia, but this is nostalgia on a small and extremely enjoyable scale. You can fill up at lunch or dinner for about $8 per person.

2. *Hollywood Brown Derby*
Terrific Cobb Salad as well as veal, pasta, and fresh seafood are served here where, not surprisingly, carica-

tures of movie stars line the walls. Service, however, is extremely slow, making this a bad choice for families with young kids. Lunch for an adult runs about $10, dinner $15.

3. *Hollywood & Vine Cafeteria of the Stars*
This large, attractive art deco restaurant offers a wide variety of salads and desserts and an outstanding rotisserie chicken. The line moves fast, and it's nice to see what you're getting. Lunch or dinner costs about $8.

FAST-FOOD PLACES AT MGM

1. *Soundstage Restaurant*
Decorated like the set of the Bette Midler–Lily Tomlin hit *Big Business,* Soundstage Restaurant is tucked away near the gate of the Animation Building and offers a small food court with pizza, soups, and sandwiches.

2. *Backlot Express*
Located near Star Tours, here's a good place for hamburgers, chicken, and hot dogs.

3. *Min & Bill's Dockside Diner*
Moored on Echo Lake, the diner serves subs and fruit plates alfresca.

4. *Studio Catering Co.*
Most people aren't aware that this restaurant, tucked away in the middle of the Backstage Studio Tour, even exists. So while the masses amble on to the second stage of the tour, you can eat a sandwich in peace.

5. *Dinosaur Gertie's*
Kids can't resist this big green tyrannosaurus, and it's a good place to get ice cream while waiting to be admitted into the Indiana Jones Epic Stunt Spectacular.

6. *Starring Rolls*

Here's your best choice for a fast breakfast. It's also a great vantage point for watching Theater of the Stars while chowing down on pastries and a staggering variety of desserts.

THE MGM DON'T MISS LIST

Everything at MGM is well done, and the park is presently small enough to comfortably tour completely in a single day.

- Star Tours
- The Great Movie Ride
- Backstage Studio Tour
- Animation Building
- Indiana Jones Epic Stunt Spectacular

THE MGM WORTH YOUR WHILE LIST

- Monster Sound Show
- SuperStar Television
- Theater of the Stars
- The Muppet Show

THE SCARE FACTOR AT MGM

The Attractions

The Great Movie Ride

This ride begins innocently enough as you drift past re-creations of scenes from classic films. But everyone in my tram, no matter what their age, gave a collective gasp when one movie set "turned real" and our tram driver was killed in a 1930s-style gangsterland shoot-out. After collecting the jewelry of a couple of the riders, the gangster commandeered our tram for the rest of the ride. "Is this supposed to be happening?" wailed one boy who looked about 7, echoing the thoughts, no doubt, of many of the riders. Danger lurks throughout the ride in the form of the alien from the movie of the same name and the green-faced Wicked Witch of the East who appears in a cloud of quite convincing mist.

Final verdict: A couple of scenes are startling and intense, and this ride will have your family debating "How did they do that?" for weeks afterward. Although aspects may scare kids under 5, the fact that the tram driver eventually reappears does underscore the fact that it's all "only pretend."

Catastrophe Canyon

As part of the Backstage Studio Tour, you experience how artificial disasters are created in an outdoor set. Your tram shakes with an earthquake and narrowly misses being swept away by a flood and rockslide. Then a fire breaks out.

Final verdict: The tour guide explains how it's all done. Most children find the canyon the most fun part of the Backstage Tour.

Monster Sound Show

Don't be put off by the title. There's a really funny film starring Chevy Chase and Martin Short, with volunteers from the audience providing sound effects.

Final verdict: Not scary at all.

Star Tours

The warnings posted at the entryway are a bit paranoid, for most kids love this attraction, especially if they've seen the *Star Wars* movie series.

Final verdict: Fine for anyone over 3.

MGM OR UNIVERSAL STUDIOS?

Proving once again that imitation is the sincerest form of flattery, Universal and Disney-MGM opened studio theme parks a scant 18 months apart. Both parks offer mind-blowing technology, are small enough to be seen in a day, and are a darn lot alike. For direct comparisons of their offerings, consider the following points to determine which park you should visit.

A Glimpse Behind the Scenes

At MGM, the backstage tour begins with a tram ride through costuming, scenery, and a special effects studio. At Universal, you walk, which allows you more time to study the details.

At MGM you visit huge outdoor sets, à la Anywhere USA. Universal takes you to Fisherman's Wharf, 1930s Chicago, and the Bates Motel.

Special effects are really special at MGM's Catastrophe Canyon, where your tram is stalled, shaken by an earthquake, blasted by an oil-tank explosion, and finally flooded. At Universal's Kongfrontation, everyone's favorite ape seizes your car and, when distracted by a helicopter, suddenly drops you. You'll get to watch your reaction via instant video replay.

Sci-Fi

In Star Tours, Disney and George Lucas bring you state-of-the-art flight-simulation technology; Universal and Steven Spielberg team up to take visitors on a bike ride with ET, this time using flight simulation to help the cuddly alien save his home planet. In perhaps the most impressive touch of all, ET bids you goodbye by name at the end of the flight.

Cartoons

Disney takes you inside an animation studio to watch artists at work. Universal's Funtastic World of Hanna-Barbera plunges you into the middle of a high-speed cartoon chase.

Witness On-Site Filming

Many of the Disney channel shows are in year-round production at the MGM park, most notably the "All New Mickey Mouse Club." Universal answers with Nickelodeon, the only network exclusively for kids, giving young tourists the chance to visit the set of that venerable classic "Super Sloppy Double Dare."

Live Action

The Great Movie Ride at MGM employs both actors and Audio-Animatronics to bring scenes from movie classics to life. Ghostbusters at Universal uses live action to explain the elaborate—and sometimes gross—special effects of that popular film.

At MGM's SuperStar Television, cast members selected from the audience star on screen with actors from "Gilligan's Island," "I Love Lucy," and "Cheers." At Universal's Screen Test Adventure, you can star in your own film and walk away with a videotape souvenir.

Getting Scared

Universal pays tribute to the master in Hitchcock: The Art of Making Movies and demonstrates how the classic film monsters got so ghoulish in Phantom of the Opera Horror Makeup Show. MGM plays horror for laughs in the Monster Sound Show, where audience volunteers add sound effects to a film starring Chevy Chase and Martin Short. Universal visitors itching to get their hands on the dials can edit tapes in the Murder, She Wrote Post-Production Theater. Disney demonstrates live-action stunts in the Indiana Jones Epic Stunt Spectacular, a 20-minute show reliving highlights from the Indiana Jones movie series.

ON THE HORIZON: PLANS FOR MGM

Don't blink. The size of the MGM theme park will double in the next 5 years.

1. Coming in 1990: The Dick Tracy Musical Revue, which will use makeup magic to bring Pruneface, the Blank, and other overlords of the underworld to the Theatre of the Stars.

2. Coming in 1990: "Let's Make a Deal," an updated version of the game show classic, will be filmed regularly, using WDW visitors as contestants.

3. Coming in 1991: Disney Channel Auditions will allow guests to not only watch auditions in prog-

ress but have the chance to put their own talents to the test. The winning screen test each day will be shown on the Disney channel, and selected guests may even win roles in future Disney productions. It's your shot at show biz!

4. Coming in 1991: It's the Honey I Shrunk the Kids Adventure Zone, where "miniaturized" guests will scramble through a world of giant bugs, sprinklers, and blades of grass. Bound to be, ahem, a big kid pleaser.

5. Coming in 1991: A 3-D Muppet film, the last project designed by the late Jim Henson. In 1993, the Muppets Movie Ride will open, bound to be one of the major MGM attractions. It's billed as "a misguided tour through movie history, offering inimitable interpretations of the greatest scenes ever seen on the silver screen—Muppet style."

6. Coming in 1992: Famed Broadway composer Andrew Lloyd Webber will join the team of Disney collaborators with his musical Noah's Ark, the most ambitious nighttime spectacle ever planned for a Disney theme park.

7. Coming in 1995: The size of MGM will expand dramatically with the opening of Sunset Boulevard, a companion street to Hollywood Boulevard. Along with restaurants and shops, expect to find:

• Toontown Trolley, a Roger Rabbit-based thrill ride.

• Benny the Cab Ride, designed for younger Rabbit fans. (The little taxis will really talk, wink, and wiggle.)

• Baby Herman's Runaway Buggy Ride, where guests will board oversized buggies and careen down stairs, through doors, and over beds.

- Dick Tracy's Crime Stoppers will take you on a high-speed chase in vintage cars through the gangland streets of Chicago. Ready to rat-a-tat? Crime Stoppers promises to "combine the excitement of a thrill ride with the challenge of a shooting gallery."

- Mickey's Movieland will give guests a chance to try out movie-making equipment and direct their own films.

7

★ ★ ★ ★ ★ ★ ★ ★ ★ ★ ★ ★ ★ ★ ★ ★ ★ ★ ★

*The Rest of
the World*

PLEASURE ISLAND

"It's New Year's Eve every night!" is the theme at Disney's Pleasure Island Nightclub Theme Park. This complex of clubs, restaurants, and shops comes alive at 7 P.M. each evening as adults 18 and over pay one admission price for unlimited entry to two dance clubs, two comedy clubs, a country and western music bar, and an alternative music bar. A different featured band puts on an 11 P.M. show each evening, winding down just before midnight, when a street party culminates in the New Year's Eve countdown, complete with champagne, fireworks, and confetti.

Pleasure Island has undergone substantial pricing and policy changes since it debuted in 1989, and to some degree Disney is still tinkering with the concept. Originally several types of tickets were offered: You could buy one, two, or all-club passes, depending on how many bars you planned to hop. Also, in the original plan, teenagers were allowed into two of the clubs, which were alcohol-free and featured youth-oriented music and entertainment. Being able to take teenagers along was nice for many families, but ensuring that the kids didn't get into the drinking clubs and handling all those different types of tickets ultimately proved too complicated for the Disney people.

In its latest incarnation, Pleasure Island is purely for adults over 18, and one $10 Island admission has replaced the ticketing system. Most patrons prefer this system; you don't have to preguess how many clubs you'll want to visit in an evening, and the single admission pass makes it easier to go from club to club, revisiting favorites several times.

Pleasure Island Touring Tips

1. If you choose Pleasure Island for a parents' night out, get an in-room sitter for the kids. Most hotel ser-

vices close down at midnight, and if you stay for the fire-works and street party, you won't be back until after that. With an in-room sitter the kids can go to bed at their usual hour. [If your hotel doesn't provide in-room sitting, call Fairy Godmothers at (407) 277-3724 before you leave home.]

2. Visit Pleasure Island after your least demanding touring day. There's not much walking at the island, but dancing is murder on already puffy feet.

3. Don't plan on eating in the clubs; most don't serve anything more elaborate than popcorn. If you arrive around 7 P.M. and the clubs haven't heated up yet, try some barbecue at the Fireworks Factory or a salad at Merriweather's Market. If you crave a fancier meal, visit the Portobello Yacht Club for Italian or the *Empress Lilly* riverboat for really elegant continental cuisine. Both establishments are located in the Disney Village Marketplace, adjacent to Pleasure Island.

4. Be aware that you won't be pressured to drink in the clubs, but if you do drink, the alcohol is expensive. Unless you opt for the "drink of the day," which costs $1.50 or $2, most drinks are $5 or more.

5. Even if you don't dance, Pleasure Island is worth-while. Nearby barstools let you watch the dancers, and the comedy clubs and live bands are very good.

Pleasure Island Touring Plan

1. Arrive about 7 P.M. Either eat at the Disney Village Marketplace before you enter, or grab something fast at Merriweather's Market or the Fireworks Factory.

2. Take in the Comedy Warehouse first. (The dance clubs don't gear up until later.) This 1-hour show, a combination of improvisation and Disney spoofs,

is proof positive that comedy doesn't have to be profane or vulgar to be funny.

3. Move to the Neon Armadillo across the street for country and western music with a live band.

4. For something completely different, try the Adventurers Club, a lavish, eccentric hideaway based on British hunting clubs of the 1930s. You won't be in the bar for long before you realize that some of your fellow drinkers are actors . . . and the masks on the walls are moving. But stay seated. Every 30 minutes or so you'll be ushered into the Treasure Room for a comic seance.

   The Adventurers Club is definitely worth an hour of your evening. There's nothing like this back home, unless you're from the Congo.

5. Next, stop by the Cage, the alternative music club, which is full of video screens and draws the most interesting crowds of any Pleasure Island club.

6. Finally, divide your remaining hours between the two dance clubs. XYFR offers a live band and nostalgic music; Mannequins is darker and wilder and features canned music, strobe lighting, and a tricky revolving dance floor.

7. Be sure to be back outside by 11 P.M. for the street party and countdown to New Year's.

8. Then grab a cappuccino and sit in the cobblestone courtyard at D-Zertz. You may feel like dancing more, or you may feel like heading home to the kids.

DISCOVERY ISLAND

A short ride across Bay Lake is thoroughly unmodern, uncrowded Discovery Island, an 11½-acre zoological park where you'll find walking trails, lush natural vegetation, beaches perfect for picnicking, and hundreds of varieties of animal life. Of special interest are the trained birds at Parrots Perch and the Galapagos sea turtles at Tortoise Beach.

Discovery Island launches leave from the MK, Fort Wilderness Campground Resort, River Country, and all the MK resorts. If you have a 5-day passport that allows you unlimited access to the minor theme parks, you may enjoy an hour or two at Discovery Island. Otherwise, don't spend the time and money ($7.50 for adults, $3 for kids 3–9) to visit the island; similar zoological parks are undoubtedly closer to your home.

Note: Kids taking the Wonders of Walt Disney World program A True-Life Adventure will spend a very productive afternoon on the island learning about the conservation of natural plant and animal habitats.

RIVER COUNTRY

Billed as an "ol' swimming hole perfect for splashin' and slidin'," River Country has been completely overshadowed by the 1989 opening of the much larger and more high-tech Typhoon Lagoon. But River Country remains the better choice of the Disney water parks for families with young kids or anyone who doesn't swim very well. River Country features an enormous pool surrounded by man-made boulders designed for jumping and diving, as well as swing ropes, two water slides, and White Water Rapids, a leisurely inner tube ride down a winding 230-foot-long creek. Preschool age kids will enjoy the Ol' Wading Pool, and there are many good places to picnic around the beautifully landscaped grounds.

The 5-day passport lets you in gratis, but you can buy separate tickets for $12 for adults, $9 for kids.

River Country Touring Tips

1. Although the oversized swimming pool is heated, making fall and spring swimming a delight, River Country is sometimes closed during December, January, and February. Call (407) 824-4321 for details on hours of operation.

2. If you don't have a 5-day passport, buy your River Country admission tickets at either Guest Relations at your hotel or at one of the major theme parks. As the park grows crowded, management sometimes abruptly suspends ticket sales, but if you already have a ticket in hand, they'll let you in.

3. If you're staying at Fort Wilderness Campground Resort you can simply walk to River Country, which is right on the grounds. Otherwise, take the shuttle from the TTC, the launch from the MK, or drive.

TYPHOON LAGOON

Disney has dubbed its 56-acre Typhoon Lagoon the "world's ultimate water park," and the hyperbole is justified. Where else can you slide through caves, float through rain forests, and swim (sort of) with sharks? Typhoon Lagoon opened in 1989 as the largest water park in the world and was instantly so popular that it's now hard to get in. In fact, Typhoon Lagoon is so hot that slipping away from the theme parks in the afternoon to visit no longer qualifies as a getaway—the pools may be as crowded as the parks.

The good news about the popularity of Typhoon Lagoon is that River Country and the hotel pools are less busy than they were 2 years ago. Also, for anyone with a 5-day passport, the Lagoon is free. Where River Country offers the low-key ambience of a small-town swimming hole, Typhoon Lagoon provides tropical splendor as well as definitely exciting and high-tech attractions:

- Humunga Kowabunga: two water slides propel riders down a mountain and through a cave at 25 mph . . . it's a bit like riding Space Mountain without a car.

- Storm Slides: three curving slides deposit riders— none too gently—in pools below.

- Mayday Falls: whitewater tubing.

- Keelhaul Falls: a whitewater corkscrew tube ride, slower than Mayday Falls.

- Gangplank Falls: four-passenger rafts in whitewater.

- Surfing Lagoon: machine-made waves up to 6 feet high in a 2.5-acre lagoon. Perfectly designed for rafting and bodysurfing, and the waves come at 90-second intervals.

- Castaway Creek: a meandering 2,000-foot-long stream full of rafts and inner tubes. Guests simply wade out, find an empty raft, and plop down. It takes about 30 minutes to encircle the "rain forest."

- Shark Reef: a saltwater pool where snorkelers swim "among" exotic marine life, including sharks (the sharks and fish are behind plexiglass).

- Ketchakiddee Creek: a water playground sized for preschoolers, with geysers, bubblers, slides, and even a small whitewater raft ride. Lots of chairs are nearby for parents.

Typhoon Lagoon Touring Tips

1. The lagoon draws a rowdy teenage crowd, which means that young kids and unsteady swimmers

may get dunked and splashed more than they like.

2. The lagoon is extra-packed on weekends since it's a favorite with locals as well as tourists.

3. Evenings may be a better bet than afternoons. Call (407) 824-4321 for hours of operation.

4. Many visitors arrive with their swimsuits on under their shorts and shirts, which does save time. But wear your Reeboks and carry your thongs—it's a good walk from the parking lot.

5. Don't bother bringing your own snorkels, rafts, or water wings because only official Disney equipment is allowed in the pools. Raft rental is $1 an hour, with a $5 deposit per family. If you arrive at the park early, you may be allowed in to rent your equipment and get outfitted before the official opening time.

6. You can pick up snorkeling equipment for free at Hammerhead Fred's near the Shark Reef. An instructor runs you through the basics before letting you loose in the saltwater pool.

7. If you want to merely watch the snorkelers and marine life, there's a viewing room beneath the pool.

8. Typhoon Lagoon is a good place for teenagers to go on their own. They can catch a shuttle from any on-site hotel or the TTC.

9. The lagoon is an excellent place to picnic.

10. Bring your own towels. Lockers are available for stashing clothes and cash.

11. Equipment rental can slow you down. Send one parent to get the rafts while the other swabs down the kids with SPF 24.

12. Typhoon Lagoon offers wilder experiences than any of the major parks, and some restrictions do apply. You must be 4 feet tall to ride Humunga Kowabunga, Mayday Falls, or Keelhaul Falls. Kids of any age are allowed on the Zesty Storm Slides and, if with their parents, on the Gang-plank Falls. Although the surfing lagoon lets anyone in, don't take the kids too deep because every 90 seconds 100 shrieking teenagers clutching rafts will bear down on your head.

DISNEY EXTRAS: THE PARADES, FIREWORKS, AND SHOWS

Don't pack your schedule too tightly. Disney works many wonderful extras into the day, and it would be downright criminal to miss them.

1. Parades: If you love a parade, you've come to the right place. Included among the festivities are the

- 3 P.M. character parade at the MK.
- Main Street Electrical Parade at 9 P.M. and 11 P.M. during the on-season.
- Electric Water Pageant, visible from the beaches of the Seven Seas Lagoon from 9–10:20 nightly.
- Special parades sometimes planned at Epcot and MGM. Consult your daily entertainment schedule for times.
- Mind-blowing holiday parades at Easter, Thanksgiving, and Christmas.

2. Fireworks: A 5–10-minute display is seen in the sky above Cinderella Castle at 10 P.M. during the on-season. Fireworks close the day yearround at MGM and Pleasure Island.

3. IllumiNations: Don't miss this laser light extravaganza at closing time each evening in Epcot.

4. Marshmallow Marsh Excursion: You leave from Fort Wilderness Campground Resort and paddle via canoe down the shadowy canals around Bay Lake, finally disembarking and hiking to a campsite for singalongs and a marshmallow roast. The Electrical Water Pageant is visible from the beach. $6 for adults, $5 for kids. Call (407) 824-2788 for reservations.

5. Campfire singalongs at Meadow Trading Post in Fort Wilderness are also a nice way to end the day.

6. The hour-long hayrides that leave Pioneer Hall in Fort Wilderness each evening are quite popular. Call (407) 824-2900 for times.

7. Dinner shows: Book all dinner shows well in advance (dialing W-DISNEY). Reservations are accepted months in advance for on-site guests, 30 days in advance for off-site guests, and are especially crucial for the Hoop-Dee-Doo Musical Revue. The three shows are

- Hoop-Dee-Doo Musical Revue. By far the best and most popular of the Disney dinner shows, the revue plays three times nightly (5, 7:30, and 10 P.M.) at Pioneer Hall in Fort Wilderness. You'll dine on ribs and fried chicken while watching a hilariously hokey show full of the kind of no-holds-barred dancing featured in the film *Seven Brides for Seven Brothers*. This show got a rousing "thumbs up" from families surveyed and was adored by kids as young as 4. $28 for adults, $23 for kids 12–20, and $15 for kids 3–11.

- Polynesian Revue. You'll enjoy authentic island dancing and not particularly authentic island food at this outdoor show at the Polynesian Village Resort. The two seatings are at 6:45 and 9:30 P.M. A better choice for families with young kids is Mickey's Tropical Revue, which features the characters. But it's at 4:30 P.M., which does break up the day a bit. Prices are the same as for the Hoop-Dee-Doo Musical Revue.

- Top of the World at the Contemporary Resort. This show, based on hit Broadway tunes, is adult-oriented and so is the food, which features duckling, veal, and standing rib roast. $40 for adults, $18 for kids 3–11. Seatings are at 6 and 9:15 P.M.

Note: If you're staying off-site and don't want to return to the WDW grounds in the evening, or if you've waited too late to book a Disney show, be advised that Orlando is chock full of engaging family-style dinner shows. See Section 8, Disney World After Dark, for details.

8. Character breakfasts: You'll make life easier for yourself if you phone W-DISNEY for reservations before you leave home.

- *Empress Lilly* riverboat restaurant, moored between Disney Village Marketplace and Pleasure Island, is the site of Breakfast à la Disney at 9 and 10:30 each morning. Probably the easiest location for families staying off-site.
- Character Cafe at the Contemporary Resort serves a continuous breakfast buffet; it doesn't take reservations.
- Minnie's Menehune at the Papeete Bay Verandah at the Polynesian Village Resort also serves a continuous buffet from 7:45 to 10:00 each morning but does accept reservations.
- Try Chip and Dale's Country Morning Jamboree at Pioneer Hall in Fort Wilderness. Showtimes are 8 and 9:45 A.M.

THAT SPORTIN' LIFE: IN THE WATER

1. Water Sprites: Those zippy little speedboats you see darting around the Buena Vista and Seven Seas Lagoons can be rented for $11 an hour. Drivers must be 12 years old, although kids of any age will enjoy riding alongside mom and pop. *Note:* The boats don't actually go very fast.

You can rent Water Sprites at the marinas of the Polynesian, Contemporary, Grand Floridian, and Fort Wilderness resorts. If you're staying off-site, it's probably easier to rent one at the Buena Vista Lagoon between the Disney Village Marketplace and Pleasure Island.

2. Sailboats: The marinas of the Polynesian, Contemporary, Grand Floridian, and Fort Wilderness resorts also have for rent sailboats ranging from the three-person Sunfish for $10 an hour to the six-person Capri for $15 an hour.

3. Pontoon boats: If your party is larger or less adventurous, try touring the Seven Seas Lagoon in a motor-powered pontoon for $35 an hour. Similar canopy boats are available at Buena Vista Lagoon for $18 per ½ hour.

4. Pedal boats: These small people-powered crafts can be rented at both the Buena Vista Lagoon and Seven Seas Lagoon for $8 an hour.

5. Canoes: If you'd like to try fishing in the canals around Fort Wilderness, rent a canoe for $4 an hour or $9 a day at the Bike Barn.

6. Outrigger canoes: Surely the wildest looking of all WDW watercraft, six people can go native in one of these Hawaiian-style canoes for $12 an hour. Available only at the Polynesian Village Resort marina.

7. Waterskiing: You can reserve boats complete with driver and full equipment up to 3 days in advance by dialing the Contemporary Resort marina at (407) 824-1000. The cost is $65 an hour.

8. Fishing: Fishing is permitted in the canals—but not the lagoons or lakes—around Fort Wilderness. Rods and reels are for rent at the Bike Barn, and you can either drop a line from shore or take a canoe or pontoon boat deeper into the canals.

9. Swimming: All the WDW hotels have private pools, but the Contemporary Resort pool is best for serious swimmers. Guests staying off-site can either return to their hotels for a dip or check out River Country or Typhoon Lagoon.

THAT SPORTIN' LIFE: ON LAND

1. Tennis: The Contemporary Resort has six courts and offers both tennis clinics and private lessons. Courts are also available at The Disney Inn, the Disney Village Resort Villas, and Fort Wilderness Campground Resort. To reserve a court 24 hours in advance, call

Contemporary Resort (407) 824-3578

The Disney Inn (407) 824-1469

Disney Village Resort Villas (407) 824-3741

The tennis courts at Fort Wilderness operate on a first-come first-serve basis.

2. Golf: There are three courses actually on the WDW grounds, with greens fees running about $55 for WDW hotel guests and about $60 for those staying off-site. To reserve a tee-off time at either the Palm or Magnolia

courses, which are behind The Disney Inn, or the Lake Buena Vista Golf Course behind the Disney Village Resort, dial (407) 824-2270. To arrange clinics or private lessons, call (407) 824-2250. WDW guests can make tee-off and lesson reservations up to 30 days in advance; those staying off-site can (and should) make reservations 7 days in advance.

3. Junior golf: Adjacent to the Magnolia course lies Wee Links, a six-hole beginner course designed for young people. The $7 fee for kids under 18 includes clubs and two rounds of play. Adults can play along for $9.

4. Running: Jogging trails cut through the grounds of nearly every WDW hotel. Consult Guest Services for a map. Fort Wilderness has a 2.3-mile exercise trail complete with posted period stops for chin-ups, sit-ups, and a host of other tortures.

5. Horseback riding: Guided trail rides leave the Fort Wilderness grounds at 9 and 10:30 A.M., noon, and 2 P.M. daily. Surprisingly and disappointingly, children under 9 are forbidden, even though the horses are gentle and the pace is slow. Call W-DISNEY for reservations before you leave home.

6. Spas: For a $4 fee you can pump a little iron at the Contemporary Resort spa, and individual whirlpools can be rented for an additional $5. The health club at the Grand Floridian Resort offers aerobics classes and Nautilus equipment for guests only.

7. Biking: You can rent bikes ($2.50 an hour) or tandems ($3 an hour) at the Bike Barn in Fort Wilderness or the Villa Center at the Disney Village Resorts.

8. Still have energy to burn? Get up a volleyball or basketball game at Fort Wilderness.

LIFE BEYOND DISNEY: OTHER WORTHWHILE AREA ATTRACTIONS

Sea World

Opened in 1973, the same year as the MK, Sea World is best known as the home of Shamu and the killer whales. But other exhibits are equally fascinating, such as the Penguin Encounter, where you can observe the tuxedoed charmers both above and below the ice floe and witness their startling transformation from awkward walkers to sleek swimmers. If you're too cool to like cute, try the Shark Encounter next door. The New Friends show featuring leaping dolphins and white beluga whales is especially popular with kids, as is the hilarious Sea Lions of the Silver Screen.

If you're feeling guilty about taking the kids out of school, Sea World offers 3-hour educational tours. (Quick: Can you tell the difference between a sea lion and a seal?) The Shamu rental strollers are so neat that most kids climb in without a fuss. But if the kids need to blow off some steam after a morning of shows, stop by the pirate ship at Cap'n Kid's World, where children can climb the rigging and shoot water muskets. Adults can unwind at Al E. Gator's, which offers Key West Conch Chowder, Sauteed Gator Tail, and Jamaican Jerk Pork.

Small children at Sea World welcome the numerous chances to get close to the beasties. My 2-year-old son loved hand-feeding the harmless looking but actually quite vicious seals and the vicious looking but actually quite harmless stingrays. Sea World admission is $24 for adults and $20 for kids 3–11, but numerous discount coupons can be found floating around Orlando. The park opens at 9 A.M., is virtually empty until 11 A.M., and can be comfortably toured in 5 hours. Have your hand stamped as you leave, spend the afternoon at one of the water parks, and return for the evening laser extravaganza.

Gatorland Zoo

The ambience of Gatorland Zoo is set as you enter through a giant blue concrete gator mouth. While most of the thousands of alligators within are rendered passive by the Florida sun, things do perk up four times a day at the Gator Jumparoo, where the gators leap as high as 5 feet out of the water to retrieve whole chickens from the trainers' hands. One young cynic surveyed pointed out that the animals jump highest at the first show of the day, aka "breakfast."

You can easily tour this campy little place, which also has a small zoo and a train ride, in a couple of hours. And while Sea World certainly doesn't serve dolphin, the Gatorland Zoo has no qualms about biting the hand that feeds it. You can pick up a few cans of Gator Chowder at the gift shop, surely a unique "thank you" for those neighbors back home who are watering the plants while you're away. The cost is $7 for adults, $5 for kids.

Wet 'n Wild

This was the original water theme park in Orlando, and in terms of sheer thrills, the preteen crowd surveyed claim it's still the best. The six-story plunge of the Der Stuka and the twisting tubes of the Niagara are not for the faint of heart. Small children and others who are chicken of the sea can slide along the Bubble Up or float down the Lazy River in big rubber tubes. The atmosphere doesn't stack up to the Huck Finn feel of Disney's River Country or the tropical splendor of Typhoon Lagoon, but Wet 'n Wild is a good place to cool off without getting back into the mouse race.

Admission is $15 for adults, $13 for kids 3–12, but your best bet is to arrive after 3 P.M., when prices drop. (Discounts don't take effect until 5 P.M. in summer, but the park stays open until midnight then.)

Mystery Fun House

Accurately described by one family as "cheesier than Velveeta," the Mystery Fun House is full of mazes, sloping floors, and optical illusions. Admission is $7 for adults, $6 for kids. A good choice only for very rainy days or very desperate parents.

Universal Studios

Here to give MGM a run for your money, Universal offers attractions dedicated to ET, King Kong, the Ghostbusters, and other characters from famed films. For a detailed comparison of MGM and Universal, see the discussion MGM or Universal Studios? in Section 6.

In addition to Orlando attractions, there are Cypress Gardens to the south, Cape Canaveral to the east, and Busch Gardens to the west, all worthwhile and all within a 1½-hour drive.

8

★★★★★★★★★★★★★★★★★★★

Disney World After Dark

DISNEY WORLD AFTER DARK: WITH THE KIDS

Is there life in the World after 8 P.M.? Sure there is. The crowds thin, the temperature drops, and many attractions are especially dazzling by dark. The particular kind of fun you'll have depends on whether or not the kids are with you. If you decide to schedule at least one parents' night out during your trip, the on-site hotels offer an enchanting array of child care options. Where else on earth can your child be bedded down by a flesh and blood Mary Poppins? Sitters can be arranged for off-site hotels as well, and some Orlando restaurants—which happen to be located in hotels with child care centers—even provide free sitting services for couples dining in their flagship restaurants.

Evening Activities for the Whole Family

1. *The night parades*
During summer months, the famous Main Street Electrical Parade runs at 9 P.M. and 11 P.M. Themes from the great Disney musicals are piped through the park P.A. system as 27 floats, aglitter with over 1 million tiny Christmas lights, stream by. Cinderella is always a major hit, as is Alice on her mushroom. If the kids can handle the wait, the 11 P.M. parade is far less crowded than the earlier one, and you also avoid the mass exodus toward the front gate after the 9 P.M. show.

2. If you're staying on-site, the Electrical Water Pageant may actually float by your hotel window since it's staged on the Seven Seas Lagoon that connects the Polynesian Village, Contemporary, Grand Floridian, and Fort Wilderness resorts. Times do vary with the seasons, so dial 11 for Guest Relations at your hotel, but

generally the Pageant is visible at 9 P.M. at the Polynesian, 9:20 from the Grand Floridian, 9:45 from Fort Wilderness, and 10:05 from the Contemporary. If you aren't staying on-site, simply ride the monorail to the resort of your choice. The Electrical Water Pageant plays every night, even during the off-season.

Especially striking vantages are at the Top of the World Lounge in the Contemporary Resort and the beach at the Polynesian Village Resort. Although this is a much shorter show than the Main Street Electrical Parade, nothing can beat the effect of multicolored lights twinkling on darkened water. Besides, by 9 P.M. most kids would rather sprawl on a beach than camp on a curb.

3. *Movies*

If you're staying on-site, check out the offerings in the Contemporary Resort's theater. Two different Disney classics show each night at 7 and 9 P.M. Admission is $1. Movies are also shown at the evening campfire at Fort Wilderness, and in many Orlando hotels the Disney channel is available 24 hours a day.

The 10-screen theater adjacent to Pleasure Island is a good place to park older kids while parents try out the clubs.

4. *Arcades*

It's no secret that kids flip for arcades, especially the mammoth Fiesta Fun Center in the Contemporary Resort. Even hardcore pinball junkies are bound to find games they've never seen before.

5. *IllumiNations at Epcot*

You can view IlluniNations from anywhere around the World Showcase Lagoon at Epcot closing time. With fireworks, laser lights, stirring music, and even choreographed fountains spurting in three-quarter time, IllumiNations is state of the art. *Note:* The fireworks are loud enough to frighten some children.

6. *Fireworks*
You can watch a rousing fireworks display from anywhere in the MK about 10 P.M. during the on-season. The show is short—although it packs a lot of punch—but at holiday times a more extensive fireworks extravaganza is presented. Fireworks also close MGM and Pleasure Island each night.

7. *Rides at night*
Those attractions with the 2-hour lines at noon are far more accessible by night, so it's worth revisiting any ride you passed by earlier in the day. In the MK, the Big Thunder Mountain Railroad is much more fun in the dark, and Cinderella's Carrousel is especially magical at night.

At Epcot, it's almost always easy to tour the Journey into Imagination and see *Captain EO* after 7 P.M. (In fact, you can easily board any Future World attraction during the dinner hour, when everyone heads out to dine in the World Showcase.) In MGM, try SuperStar Television or the Indiana Jones Epic Stunt Spectacular.

Dinner Shows for the Whole Family

Disney isn't the only company in Orlando offering family dinner theaters. The shows now described are very much alike; five of them offer a four-course meal, unlimited beer and wine, and a live show. (Prices run about $25 for adults, $16 for kids.) There is one seating nightly in the halls, which hold 400 to 1,000 people, so come prepared to buddy up to that couple from Michigan.

1. *Arabian Nights*
The only dinner show to serve prime rib (although the

food is only so-so at all these places), Arabian Nights features more than 60 horses, including white lipizzans and a "mystical unicorn." The highlight of the evening is a high-speed chariot race re-created from the movie *Ben Hur*.

2. *Fort Liberty*

The favorite of younger kids, this Wild West show offers Indian rain dances, lasso exhibitions, and the wacky denizens of Professor Gladstone's Medicine Show. Barbecue, fried chicken, and corn on the cob are served up chuck wagon style.

3. *Medieval Times*

Dueling swordsmen and jousting knights on horseback perform in a huge pit while guests dine on roast chicken and ribs. Several of the gentlemen surveyed gave a "must see" rating to the serving wenches' costumes.

4. *Mardi Gras*

Smaller and a bit more distinctive than the others, Mardi Gras is a highly sanitized version of a New Orleans show, complete with cancan dancers and a Dixieland band. The food is less spicy than French Quarter fare too; expect fried shrimp and tenderloin.

5. *King Henry's Feast*

The portly monarch is searching for his seventh wife—portraits of her six unlucky predecessors hang in the entry hall—as magicians, jugglers, and fire-eaters offer a kinder, gentler version of Medieval Times. Chicken and ribs are on hand for the revelers.

If you neglected to book a dinner show before you left home, it is generally possible to make reservations for one of the nonDisney shows on the same day you wish to attend. Reservations are generally taken from noon to 4 P.M.

WITHOUT THE KIDS

Getting Sitters

1. If your kids are exhausted, you're traveling with a baby, or you plan to be out until midnight, have a sitter come to your hotel room. KinderCare provides trained sitters for all the Disney hotels, if you call (407) 827-5444 at least 8 hours in advance. Sometimes, if you and your spouse would like to play golf or tennis, for example, in-room sitters are available in the afternoon; the rate is $6 an hour for two kids.

At least three independent services in town dispatch sitters to off-site hotels:

MOMS (407) 857-7447

Super Sitters (407) 740-5516

Fairy Godmothers (407) 277-3724

These services stay busy during the summer months, so it's not a bad idea to book them before you leave home. Rates are typically about $6 an hour, with a 4-hour minimum and an extra child charge of $1 an hour per child.

Of the independent services, Fairy Godmothers is the most inclusive, with service available 24 hours a day, 7 days a week. If you're willing to pay the extra bucks, sitters will take the kids out to fast-food places for supper, or even to area attractions. One resourceful divorced father took his two daughters along on a business trip to Orlando; while he sat in meetings, a Fairy Godmother trotted the girls around the theme parks.

2. KinderCare offers a "learning while playing" developmental program for toddlers through 12-year-olds. The setup is similar to the hundreds of Kinder-Cares nationwide. Children must be toilet trained. The

center opens at 6 P.M. Call (407) 827-5444 for reservations.

3. Mouseketeer Clubhouses are at both the Contemporary [(407) 824-1000] and Grand Floridian [(407) 824-3000] Resorts. Kids 3–9 who are staying in any of the Disney hotels (not just the MK resorts) are treated to an extensive program of events, and frequently the Disney characters drop by for a visit. One mother reported that her 3-year-old daughter was highly skeptical about being left until she was greeted at the door by Alice in Wonderland, her favorite. After that there were no more tears until 4 hours later, when mom returned to pick up Jillian.

The clubhouses are well stocked with Disney-themed toys, giving the kids, unfortunately, plenty of ideas for "must have" mementos. Otherwise, on-site child care is a bargain. You pay $4 per hour for the first child; additional kids cost a mere 50 cents per hour. There's a 4-hour minimum visit, and reservations are required. The clubhouses are open from 4:30 P.M. until midnight, and cookies and milk are served at bedtime. Again, kids must be toilet trained—even Mary Poppins has her limits.

Not to be outdone, the Polynesian Village Resort offers a dinner theater for kids 3–12 at The Neverland Club, with a full meal and entertainment. The cost is $5 per child per hour, with a minimum 3-hour visit. Make reservations at (407) 824-2170. Still feel guilty about leaving them?

4. Several off-site hotels, most notably the Hilton at Disney Village Hotel Plaza, the Peabody Orlando on International Drive, and Stouffer Orlando Resort just across from Sea World, have their own version of a Kid's Club, with wide-screen TVs, Nintendo games, and wading pools to entertain the children while parents do the town.

Shamu's Playhouse at the Stouffer, named after the popular baby whale of Sea World fame, is probably the most complete and the only one open during daylight hours. Shamu's Playhouse is also the only child care center to accept infants; the Hilton and the Peabody request that kids be toilet trained. All three centers mentioned will provide simple meals for the kids at a slight extra charge. And the price is right: about $4 an hour.

The price is even better if you're dining at Dux at the Peabody, American Vineyards at the Hilton, or either Atlantis or Haifeng at Stouffer. Patrons of these premier restaurants receive 3 hours of complimentary child care, and this service isn't limited to guests of the hotel. (For more information, see the Off-Site Hotels: Great Places for Families discussion in Section 2.)

Child care is a subject near to the heart of many Orlando visitors, and hotels are catching on fast, so other establishments are bound to offer their own Kid's Clubs soon. In the meantime, reservations are best made in advance.

Peabody Orlando (407) 352-4000

Stouffer Orlando Resort (407) 351-5555

Hilton at Disney Village Hotel Plaza (407) 827-4000

DINING

Certain on-site restaurants are more enjoyable without the children along. After you've found a sitter, reserve a table for two at one of these establishments.

Epcot Center

1. *Chefs de France or the Bistro de Paris*

Chefs de France features nouvelle cuisine, meaning that the sauces are lighter and the preparation simpler than traditional French fare. This is still heady stuff: grouper with lobster sauce, roast duckling with prunes, salmon and tarragon souffle. The atmosphere is elegant and understated and the service unrushed. Chefs is definitely one of the most expensive eateries in Epcot, with dinner running about $100 for two.

The Bistro de Paris (upstairs) is slightly less pricey and just as good. The atmosphere is lovely—high ceilings, brass, and etched glass abound—with attentive service and hearty, casual French dining. Waiters are more than willing to advise you on selections and, as is true at Chefs, it's impossible to go wrong with any of the desserts.

2. *Marrakesh*

Ready to take a walk on the semiwild side? The music, architecture, and menu in this Moroccan restaurant are truly distinctive, proving beyond a doubt that you aren't in Kansas anymore. You'll be served by waiters in floor-length robes while belly dancers weave among the tile tables. (The effect of these dancers on husbands is somewhat akin to the effect of meeting Mickey on toddlers—they're stunned while it's happening but later remember the experience fondly.)

Since you're probably not familiar with Moroccan cuisine, try the sampler platters, which offer tastes of skewered veal, couscous, honeyed chicken, and thin pastries filled with lamb.

3. *San Angel Inn Restaurante*

The menu here goes far past the tacos and enchiladas most Americans consider Mexican, and the atmosphere is unparalleled. The restaurant overlooks El Rio del Tiempo, the boat ride that encircles an Aztec pyramid beneath a starry sky. The darkness of the Mexico pavilion, which simulates midnight even at high noon, and the murmur of the Rio are hypnotic. Throw in a couple of margaritas and you may never leave.

The mole poblano and any of the grilled seafood dishes are consistently terrific. The friendliness of the service makes the San Angel a good choice even when the children are along.

4. *L'Originale Alfredo di Roma Ristorante*

The Alfredo in question is the gentleman who created fettucine Alfredo, and this is the most popular restaurant in Epcot, usually the first to book up even though it seats 250 people. The restaurant in itself is entertaining: You can watch the cooks crank out pasta through a large window; the walls are adorned with clever trompe l'oeil murals; and the waiters and waitresses provide impromptu concerts, ranging from mildly bawdy Italian folksongs to Verdi.

But perhaps Alfredo's has become too hot. Before the Coral Reef Restaurant opened in 1988, Alfredo's was the toast of Epcot, and the chefs received a good deal of media attention. Diners complained that the quality of the food became unpredictable and the service lax. Some families rate Alfredo's as their favorite Epcot choice, but others are profoundly disappointed. This is maybe a better choice for lunch than dinner.

5. *Coral Reef Restaurant*

Tucked away under The Living Seas, this Future World restaurant is also expensive, about $100 for a couple at dinner. Unfortunately, the Coral Reef is less romantic than the World Showcase restaurants. The room is simply too large to feel cozy, and most families bring their kids, figuring—and rightly so—that little Nathaniel and Erica can stay busy watching the skindivers while mom and dad crack a lobster.

Outside Epcot Center

At least two places in the World are so elegant and so removed from the classic Disney image that you'll never feel sticky fingers creeping over the top of the booth behind you. Kids are rarely seen at the following establishments, which require ties and jackets for men and something other than jeans for women.

1. *Victoria and Albert's*
(at the Grand Floridian Resort)

Where Disney has built a reputation on providing pleasure to the masses, this 50-seat restaurant proves that there's also room in the World for highly individualized service. When Henry Flagler built the railroad that opened Florida to the oil magnates of the late 1800s, Queen Victoria and Prince Albert sat upon the British throne. Now, in one of those "only Disney would go to such trouble" details, all hosts and hostesses in the restaurant are named either Victoria or Albert.

There's no printed menu at Victoria and Albert's; waiters describe the selections for the evening, and the chef often circulates among the tables. At the end of a four-course meal, guests are presented with long-stemmed roses, Godiva chocolates, and handwritten souvenir menus. Call (407) 824-2391 for reservations.

Note: Victoria and Albert's is the only full-service restaurant in WDW not included in the Gold Passkey or any other package dining plans. Dinner for two will cost about $150.

2. *The Empress Room,* aboard the *Empress Lilly* riverboat at the Disney Village Marketplace

It's fun to board this permanently moored reproduction of an 1880s steamwheeler. The *Empress Lilly* actually contains three restaurants, ranging from the casual New Orleans-style jazz bar of Fisherman's Quarters to the elegant Louis XV decor of the Empress Room. In contrast to Victoria and Albert's, the Empress Room offers a large menu, with the emphasis on seafood. Unusual dishes such as venison, pheasant, and quail are also available, and the service is top-notch, although a little less personalized than Victoria and Albert's.

You can make reservations up to 30 days in advance by calling (407) 828-3900; in the summer you'll need to make them that early. The Empress Room seats no guests after 9:30, so plan accordingly. Pleasure Island is a short walk after you finish.

3. If you'd like to slip away for a cocktail, try the Top of the World Lounge at the Contemporary Resort. Although the food and Broadway dinner show in the adjacent restaurant are nothing special, the view from the lounge is lovely indeed. Here's a perfect place to sip Cabernet after a hard day of World touring.

4. Excellent dining abounds beyond the Disney World gates. You might want to try Royal Orleans in the Mercado Shopping Center on International Drive for outstanding creole and cajun food, much of it prepared tableside. Dux in the Peabody Orlando offers an intimate environment, unusual seafood and game selections, and an outstanding list of California wines, many available by the glass. Dining of a campier sort is at Church Street Station, where Rosie O'Grady's and Lili Marlene's dish up tasty but casual food, huge specialty drinks, and live music.

5. If you still have the strength to dance, visit Pleasure Island; see Section 7 for details.

9

★ ★ ★ ★ ★ ★ ★ ★ ★ ★ ★ ★ ★ ★ ★ ★ ★ ★

And Another Thing . . .

BARE NECESSITIES: DIAPERS, STROLLERS, BABY CARE CENTERS, AND OTHER INFORMATION

Picky Eaters

1. Try the cafeterias: the Crystal Palace in the MK, Le Cellier in the Canada pavilion at Epcot, and Hollywood & Vine Cafeteria of the Stars at MGM.

2. Several of the on-site hotels run buffets in the interest of moving people in and out fast, but they're also a draw for families who can't agree on what to eat. 1900 Park Fare at the Grand Floridian Resort and the Terrace Cafe at the Contemporary Resort are both good choices.

3. Nearly all the theme park restaurants offer such standards as peanut butter and jelly, albeit at $3 a sandwich. Ask to see the kiddie menu at the door.

Strollers

1. All kids under 3 need a stroller, for napping and waiting in line as well as riding.

2. For kids 3–6, the general rule is: Strollers are a must at Epcot, nice at the MK, and not really needed at MGM, where the park is smaller and lots of time is spent in sit-down shows.

3. Strollers rent for $5 a day, with $1 refunded when you return the stroller as you leave the park. If you plan to spend time at more than one park, you don't have to pay twice: Keep your receipt and show it for a new stroller when you arrive at the next park.

4. Some families bring their own strollers instead of renting them, thus saving the $4 a day.

5. The MK and Epcot strollers are sturdy, drop back to form a completely flat bed, and can hold two kids in a pinch. The MGM strollers are the easily collapsible sling style.

6. Stolen stroller? Check in at the Space Port in Tomorrowland, the Frontier Trading Post in Frontierland, or Tinkerbell Toy Shop at Fantasyland in the MK. Or get a new stroller at France, Germany, and United Kingdom pavilions at Epcot and return it to Oscar's Classic Car Souvenirs & Super Service Station on Hollywood Boulevard at MGM.

7. If at 8 A.M. your 5-year-old swears she doesn't need a stroller and then collapses in a heap halfway around Epcot's World Showcase, head for the France pavilion; if you wheedle, they'll rent you a stroller.

Baby Services

Rockers, warming bottles, high chairs, and changing tables are all found here. You can buy diapers, formula, jars of baby food, and other supplies. (One mother reported that the attendant on duty was even able to diagnose a suspicious-looking rash on her toddler as a reaction to too much citrus juice, evidently a common Florida malady. She later took the child to a doctor and learned that the attendant was right on the money.) Magic Kingdom Baby Services is beside the Crystal Palace at the end of Main Street. Baby Services is inside the Guest Services building at MGM and near the Odyssey Restaurant at Epcot.

Breast-Feeding

WDW is so casual and family oriented that you shouldn't feel self-conscious about discreetly nursing in the theaters or restaurants. Some shows, like The Hall of Presidents in MK or *Impressions de France* in Epcot, are dark, quiet, and ideal for nursing. Others, like Country Bear Vacation Hoedown in MK or the Monster Sound Show at MGM, are so loud that the baby will probably be distracted.

If either you or your baby are too modest for these methods, try the rockers in the Baby Services areas.

Diapers

Diapers are available at

- Baby Services centers
- Stroller rental shops
- Gateway Gifts in Future World and the Centorium in CommuniCore East at Epcot
- Emporium on Main Street in MK
- Celebrity 5 & 10 in MGM

The shops don't waste valuable shelf space on such mundane products, so you'll have to ask. Changing tables are available in most ladies' restrooms. Disney, ordinarily so sensitive to family trends, has been slow to acknowledge the fact that dads change diapers, so very few men's restrooms are equipped with the necessary facilities, but fathers can always use a Baby Services center.

Special Needs

1. Wheelchairs can be rented at any stroller rental stand, and all WDW attractions are accessible by wheelchair. Attendants are happy to help guests who have special needs to board and disembark from rides.

2. Portable tape players and cassettes for sight-impaired guests are available, as are TDDs for the hearing-impaired. Check with City Hall in the MK, Earth Station at Epcot, and Guest Relations at MGM.

3. All on-site hotels are equipped to refrigerate insulin.

HOW TO GET UP-TO-DATE INFORMATION

1. If you need information before you leave home, write

   Walt Disney World Guest Information
   P.O. 10040
   Lake Buena Vista, FL 32830-0040

   Or call (407) 824-4321.

2. Subscribe to *Disney News*. You'll receive eight quarterly issues (a 2-year subscription) for $14.95. Write

   Disney News
   P.O. 3310
   Anaheim, CA 92803-3310

3. Buy a share of Disney stock and become an automatic member of the Magic Kingdom Club. You'll receive newsletters and quarterly stock reports full of great information about special trip packages and upcoming attractions.

If you need information once you check into your hotel:

1. Both on- and off-site hotels provide a wealth of material upon check in. The material is worth perusing your first evening.

2. On-site hotels provide continuous information about park operating hours, special events, and touring tips on channel 5. Hotels in the Disney World Hotel Plaza have a similar service on channel 10, and some of the large off-site hotels have their own entertainment information channels that keep you up-to-date not only on Disney but on all Orlando-area attractions.

3. MK radio is 1030 AM; Epcot is 810 AM.

4. Guest Services in both on- and off-site hotels is equipped to answer most questions.

5. If you still have questions, dial (407) 824-4321.

If you need information once you're in the parks:

1. Check with Guest Services, which is located near the main gate of all three major theme parks.

2. In Epcot, WorldKey Information Services terminals (which operate like those located under Spaceship Earth) are on the bridges that connect Future World to the World Showcase. You'll have access to a real live Disney employee within seconds.

3. You can simply flag down the nearest person wearing a Disney tag. The "cast members" at the theme parks are remarkably helpful and well-informed.

SAVING TIME

1. Do as much as you can before you leave home. You should purchase theme park tickets, reserve rental cars, and book shows long before you pull out of your driveway. Every call you make now eliminates a line to stand in later.

2. Visit the most popular attractions before 11 A.M. or after 5 P.M.

3. Eat lunch at 11 A.M., dinner as early as 4:30 or 5 P.M.; this system will have you eating while everyone else is in line for the rides and riding while everyone else is eating.

4. Split up. Mom can make the dinner reservations while dad rents the strollers. Mom can take the 9-year-old to Space Mountain while dad and the 5-year-old try out the Grand Prix Raceway. Security in WDW is very tight, so preteens and teens can tour on their own, meeting up with the rest of the family periodically.

5. Be aware that once you cross the Florida state line, there's an inverse relationship between time and money. You have to be willing to spend one to save the other. One family proudly listed among their cost-saving measures staying 30 miles outside of Orlando and cooking every meal themselves. They concluded by stating that it took them 6 days to tour the three major parks, something most families can manage comfortably in 4 days. Considering the high cost of admissions, it's doubtful that they saved very much money at all, and they certainly wasted much time.

6. If you have 3 days or less to tour, it's imperative that you go during the off-season. You can see 3 days in November what would take 6 days in July.

7. Don't feel you have to do it all. If you study this guide and your maps before you go, you'll realize that not every attraction will be equally attractive to your family. The World won't come to an end if you skip a few pavilions or attractions.

8. Service can be very slow at all of the theme park sit-down restaurants. If you're on a tight schedule, stick to fast food and sidewalk vendors.

MEETING THE DISNEY CHARACTERS

Meeting the Disney characters is a major objective for some families, and a nice diversion for all. If your children are young, be aware that the characters are much, much larger than they appear on TV and often overwhelming in person. Schedule a character breakfast on the last morning of your visit; by then cautious youngsters have usually warmed up.

Many kids enjoy getting character autographs, and an autograph book can become a much-cherished souvenir upon your return home. You also might want to prepare the kids for the fact that the characters don't talk. As many as 30 young men in Mickey suits might be dispensed around the World on a busy day, and they can't all be gifted with that familiar squeaky voice. Thus the characters communicate, and pretty effectively, through body language.

Also be aware that because of the construction of their costumes, the characters can't always see what's beneath them too clearly. Donald and Daisy, for example, have a hard time looking over their bills, and small children standing close by may be ignored. If it appears that this is happening, lift your child to the eye level of the character.

Want to actually meet the characters? To get close enough for autographs and pictures? If so, try the following locales:

- Mickey's Starland in the MK (be sure to line up to see Mickey in his dressing room after the show).
- Courtyard of Cinderella Castle in the MK (check your entertainment guide for greeting times, and be forewarned that it's crowded).
- Around the lagoon in Epcot's World Showcase.
- At the character breakfasts, of course. (See our

Best Breakfasts of the World discussion later in this section.)

- Characters sometimes appear at the restaurants in the WDW hotels (Chip and Dale, for instance, regularly circulate among diners at 1900 Park Fare in the Grand Floridian Resort). You don't have to be a guest of the hotel to dine at these restaurants.

- The Mouseketeer Clubs (the on-site sitting services at the WDW hotels) are always visited by at least one Disney character around tuck-in time. Compared to the parks, where you get a handshake and picture pose if you're lucky, these are leisurely visits.

If you want to simply *see* the characters, you have other options. Try the

- Parades—the MK has its 3 P.M. show, MGM its daily Muppet parade.

- Character shows at all three parks. There are generally lagoon shows at Epcot and the Theater of the Stars at MGM, and two different shows in the MK.

PREGNANT?

I've personally toured WDW twice while pregnant and not only lived to tell the tale but honestly enjoyed both trips. A few precautions are in order.

1. Make regular meal stops. Instead of buying a Handwich from a vendor, get out of the sun and off your feet at a cafeteria or sit-down restaurant.

2. Most pregnant women are in good condition, but if you aren't accustomed to walking 3 or 4 miles a day, which is an average WDW trek, begin getting in shape at home. Take 20- to 30-minute walks, be-

ginning a couple of months before your trip, to keep from getting sore or pooping out once you're at WDW.

3. Dehydration is a real danger. Drink lots of fluids, and consider throwing a juice box into your tote bag for emergencies.

4. This is definitely an occasion when it's worth the money to stay on-site. Return to your room in midafternoon and put your feet up.

5. If staying on-site isn't feasible, the Baby Services centers have rockers and are a good place for mothers-to-be to take a break. And the parks are full of benches, so sit whenever you have to.

6. Standing stock-still can be much more tiring than walking, so let your husband stand in line for rides. You and the kids can join him just as he's about to enter the final turn of the line.

7. See the "Best Restroom Locations in . . ." discussions in Sections 4 and 5 (pages 83 and 110).

ON A DIET?

Vacation dieting is always tough, and fast food abounds in the World, making it even more difficult. But the following restaurants offer salads, fresh fruit, and, in some cases, simply prepared dishes such as broiled seafood.

In the Magic Kingdom

- Crystal Palace, the only cafeteria in the MK, at the end of Main Street
- The Lunching Pad in Tomorrowland

- Sunshine Tree Terrace in Adventureland
- Liberty Tree Tavern in Liberty Square

In Epcot Center

- The Land Grille Room in The Land pavilion
- Farmer's Market in The Land pavilion
- The Coral Reef Restaurant under The Living Seas pavilion
- The Yakitori House in the Japan pavilion

In MGM

- Hollywood & Vine Cafeteria of the Stars
- Backlot Express

BEST BREAKFASTS OF THE WORLD

Wasn't it Archimedes who said "Give me a good breakfast and I can move the world?" These following meals will at least set you up for an active morning of touring:

- Crepes at The Land Grille Room in The Land at Epcot.
- Bagels and cream cheese at the Farmer's Market, also in The Land.
- Heart-shaped waffles with powdered sugar at Kringla Bakeri og Kafe in the Norway pavilion at Epcot.
- Stellar Scramble at the Stargate Restaurant in Epcot.
- Pastries are available throughout WDW but are especially good at

Boulangerie Patisserie in the France pavilion at Epcot.

Starring Rolls at MGM.

Main Street Bakery & Cookie Shop in the MK.

- Character waffles at Tony's on Main Street in the MK.
- Breakfast pizza at Pioneer Hall at Fort Wilderness.
- The absolute best: banana-stuffed French toast at the Coral Isle Cafe in the Polynesian Village Resort. Worth a special trip!

The food is pedestrian at the character breakfasts, but who cares? It takes a while to get your food and meet all the characters, so try to book the first seating of the day. Prices generally run about $10 for adults, $6 for children. The more elaborate Sunday brunches are also more expensive: about $17 for adults, $9 for kids.

- Breakfast à la Disney on the *Empress Lilly* riverboat at Pleasure World. This location is a snap for families staying off-site. The two seatings are at 9 A.M. and 10:30 A.M. Make reservations at (407) 828-3900.
- Character Cafe in the Contemporary Resort. A continuous seating buffet from 8–11 A.M., no reservations accepted.
- Minnie's Menehuna Breakfast at the Papeete Bay Verandah at the Polynesian Village Resort Buffet from 7:30–10:30 A.M., reservations accepted up to 30 days in advance. Call (407) 824-1391.
- Chip and Dale's Country Morning Jamboree at the Fort Wilderness Campground Resort is a breakfast show with two seatings, 8 A.M. and 9:45 A.M. Call (407) W-DISNEY for reservations.

- The Grand Floridian Cafe. A continuous seating buffet from 7–10 A.M., no reservations accepted.

THINGS YOU DON'T WANT TO THINK ABOUT

1. *Rain.* Go anyway. Short of an all-out hurricane, Disney attractions are open as usual, and crowds are thin. If you get caught in one of those afternoon cloudbursts so common during the Florida summers, rain ponchos sell for about $5 in most of the larger shops. Although hardly high fashion, they're better than trying to maneuver an umbrella through crowds, especially if you're also pushing a stroller.

2. *First aid.* Beside the Crystal Palace is a first aid center staffed with two registered nurses. Although by far most of the patients suffer from maladies such as sunburn, motion sickness, and minor boo-boos, the center is also equipped for major emergencies and, when necessary, transport to Sand Lake Hospital.

Epcot has a first aid center located at the Odyssey Restaurant; MGM's center is in the Guest Services building.

3. *Lost kids.* Obviously your best bet is to not get separated in the first place. Savvy families have standard meeting spots. (*Note:* Everyone designates Cinderella Castle or Spaceship Earth, one reason why those places are always mobbed. Plan to catch up with your crowd at a more out-of-the-way locale such as the flower stall on Main Street or the gardens beside the Canada pavilion.)

If you do get separated and your kids are too young to understand the idea of a meeting place, act fast. Lost kid logs are kept at the Baby Services centers in both

Epcot and the MK; more importantly, Disney employ-
ees are well briefed about what to do if they encounter a
lost child, so the odds are good that if your child has been
wandering around alone for more than a couple of minutes, he or she has been intercepted by a Disney employee and is on her or his way to the Baby Services
center. In real emergencies—if the child is very young
or handicapped or you're afraid the youngster has been
nabbed—All Points Bulletins are put out among em-
ployees. So if you lose a child, don't spend a ½ hour wandering around; contact the nearest Disney employee,
and let the system take it from there.

   4. *Stolen strollers.* This is a very common problem. A
family with a 4-year-old enters at 8 A.M., and everyone is
fresh and raring to go. The little boy adamantly rejects
the idea of a stroller, but by noon the kid is pooped, parents are desperate, and they emerge from Peter Pan's
Flight to find their stroller swiped. This is far more
likely to happen in the Fantasyland section of the MK
than anywhere else, where stroller parking is so congested that even honest mistakes are common. Most
families write their names on the receipt dangling from
the stroller handle, but if you go a bit further and attach
a bandana or some other marker to your stroller, you're
less likely to have yours accidentally taken.
   If your stroller is missing, go to Tinkerbell Toy Shop
in Fantasyland, the Space Port in Tomorrowland, or the
Frontier Trading Post in Frontierland—a new stroller
will be wheeled out in minutes. In Epcot, strollers are
replaced in the France, Germany, and United Kingdom
pavilions. At MGM, which is much smaller, return to
Oscar's Classic Car Souvenirs & Super Service Station
near the main gate. (As long as you keep the top half of
your receipt, your deposit will still be refunded at the
end of the day.)

5. *Auto breakdowns.* If you return to the parking lot at the end of the day to find your battery dead or some other disaster, walk back to the nearest tram stop. WDW roads are patrolled continually by security vehicles who can call for help.

The Disney Car Care Center [(407) 824-4813] is located near the toll plaza at the MK entrance. Although prices are high, the Car Care Center does provide towing and minor repairs and is your best bet in an emergency. If the car can't be swiftly repaired, don't despair; the day isn't lost because WDW personnel will chauffeur you to any theme park or back to your hotel.

By far the most common problem is forgetting where you parked. Be sure to write down your row number as you leave your car in the morning. Although it seems easy to remember now, you may not be able to retrieve that information 12 brain-numbing hours later.

6. *Running out of money.* The Sun Bank, which has branches all around WDW, gives cash advances on MasterCard and Visa and will provide refunds for lost American Express or Bank of America travelers checks. You can also cash personal checks for up to $25 (up to $1,000 if you have an American Express card) or exchange foreign currency for dollars.

SAVING MONEY

Saving money at WDW is somewhat of an oxymoron, but there are ways to contain the damage.

1. Buy Disney stock. Even owning one share qualifies you for savings of up to 40% at Disney hotels during certain seasons of the year.

2. If the cost of flying the whole family down and then renting a car is prohibitive, consider renting a van in your hometown and driving to Orlando.

3. Eat as many meals as possible outside the parks. If you have a suite, fixing simple meals there is clearly your most economical option. Many Orlando hotels offer free buffet breakfasts, and numerous fast-food and family chain restaurants are located along International Drive.

4. If you'd like to try some of the nicer Epcot restaurants, book them for lunch, when prices are considerably lower than those at dinner.

5. Except for maybe an autograph book and a T-shirt, hold off souvenir purchases until the last day. By then kids will really know what they want, and you won't waste money on impulse buys.

6. Buy your film, VCR tapes, diapers, and sunscreen at home before you come. These things are all available in the parks, but you pay dearly for the convenience.

7. The Caribbean Beach and Fort Wilderness Campground resorts provide your most economical on-site lodging. Off-site, several Comfort Inns and Days Inns are located along I-4 and International Drive; most offer shuttle service to the parks. Larger families will probably come out ahead by paying for a suite.

8. Restaurant portions are huge, even with kiddie meals. Consider letting two kids share an entree.

BEST SOUVENIRS

1. Boldly colored T-shirts featuring the flags of Epcot countries, available at Disney Traders near the mouth of the World Showcase Lagoon.

2. Autograph books, which can be purchased nearly anywhere on the first day of your trip. The signatures of the more obscure characters like Eeyore

or the Queen of Hearts are especially to be valued.

3. Characters in vehicles, purchased at the small trinket shops near the stroller rental stands. Mickey rides a movable crane, Minnie a pink roadster, Donald a locomotive, and so on; these figures are the perfect size for a toddler's chubby fist. At $3 each, they're one of the few souvenir bargains in the World.

4. Anything featuring Figment, the googly-eyed purple star of Journey into Imagination. Available throughout Future World in Epcot.

5. Disney watches, with an outstanding selection at Uptown Jewelers on Main Street in the MK. Check out the Goofy watch—it runs backward.

6. A pinata from the Mexico pavilion at Epcot.

7. Character Christmas ornaments, found in abundance at either Mickey's Christmas Carol in Fantasyland or the Christmas Chalet at the Disney Village Marketplace.

8. Anything featuring Mr. Broccoli, that punk-rocking high-fiber star of the Kitchen Kabaret in Epcot's The Land pavilion.

9. Endor Vendors, adjacent to the Star Tours ride at MGM, offers a slick selection of silver and black jackets.

10. Also at MGM, old movie posters and other campy memorabilia are sold at Sid Cahuenga's One-of-a-Kind.

11. Character cookie cutters or presses that stamp Mickey's visage onto toast and pancakes are at Yankee Trader in Liberty Square in the MK. A Disney-themed breakfast on your first Saturday home is a nice way to fight those posttrip blues.

12. Speaking of home, a 3-D Viewmaster and a handful of discs can make the return trip less painful. The best disc selection is at the Kodak Camera Center on Main Street.

13. And of course, mouse ears have a sort of retro chic. Get your name stitched on at The Mad Hatter in Fantasyland.

FAVORITE TEEN AND PRETEEN ATTRACTIONS

The following attractions received the highest approval ratings among WDW visitors 11–16.

In the Magic Kingdom

- Space Mountain (Starjets and Big Thunder Mountain Railroad are good substitutes for the faint-hearted)
- Pirates of the Caribbean
- Mad Tea Party

In Epcot Center

- *Captain EO,* the 3-D Michael Jackson film in the Journey into Imagination pavilion
- Universe of Energy
- Wonders of Life, especially the Body Wars ride
- IllumiNations
- The American Adventure

In MGM

- Star Tours (the highest-rated attraction of all!)

- Indiana Jones Epic Stunt Spectacular
- Monster Sound Show

In the Rest of the World

- Typhoon Lagoon—teenagers rated it much racier than River Country.
- Fiesta Fun Center—the mammoth game room inside the Contemporary Resort.
- Water Sprites—if you aren't staying at one of the Disney hotels that offer these minispeedboats, you can rent them at the Buena Vista Lagoon near the Disney Village Marketplace. These are a great way for the kids—and dad—to kill time while mom shops.

SNAPSHOTS YOU CAN'T LIVE WITHOUT

You can rent 35mm cameras at any of the Kodak Camera Centers for a nominal fee. Film and 2-hour photo developing are widely available throughout WDW. Needless to say, the prices of film and developing are higher than at home, but it's good to know you can get more film fast if you go into a photo frenzy.

For those postcard-perfect shots, Kodak has well-marked "photo spot" locations through all the major theme parks. But if, like most parents, what you really want to focus on is your own kids, try the following locations.

In the Magic Kingdom

1. Dumbo, just before takeoff.
2. With Cinderella, in the downstairs waiting area of King Stefan's Banquet Hall.

3. Among the cardboard stills inside the waiting area of Mickey's Starland.

4. With Mickey, of course, in his Starland tent.

In Epcot Center

1. In front of the entrance fountains or at the neat antigravity fountains at Journey into Imagination.

2. Leaning against the railings inside The Land, with hot air balloons in the background.

3. With the characters garbed in spacegear, during breakfast at the Stargate Restaurant.

4. With the characters fetchingly dressed for Mardi Gras, at the first World Showcase Lagoon show of the day.

In MGM

1. Halfway through the Backstage Studio Tour there's a break for bathrooms, snacks . . . and pictures à la *Who Framed Roger Rabbit*. The kids can even pose "beneath" the steamroller that nearly did in the ToonTown gang.

2. With your waitress-mom at the 50's Prime Time Cafe.

3. With the gossip columnist, budding starlets, autograph hounds, or other "streetmosphere" players on Hollywood Boulevard.

4. In front of Dinosaur Gertie's.

5. On the lawn of the Golden Girls' house, in the middle of Residential Street, after you take the first part of the Backstage Studio Tour.

6. Measuring your footprints against those of the

real-life stars in the concrete courtyard of the Great Movie Ride.

CAMCORDER TAPING TIPS

1. Camcorders are heavy and bulky, and it's risky leaving them in strollers while you're inside the attractions. For the sake of your back, take your camcorder with you on only one day, preferably the last day of your trip when you're revisiting favorite attractions—that way you'll leave with a "greatest hits" tape.

2. If you do plan to take your camcorder with you frequently, use the lockers located near the main gates of all three parks.

3. Don't pan and zoom too much because sudden camera moves disorient the viewer. If you're filming the kids, say, on the teacups, use the wide-angle lens and keep the camera stationary. Attempting to track them in close-ups as they spin past is too tough for anyone but a pro.

4. Camcorders can be rented at the Kodak Camera Center on Main Street in the MK or at the Camera Center near Spaceship Earth in Epcot. Rental is $40 a day, and a refundable deposit of $400 is required. (The deposit is generally taken on a credit card, and the imprint is ripped up at the end of the day when you return the camera undamaged.)

5. If you rent a camera or are borrowing one from home, try to familiarize yourself with the machine before you begin actually filming. Novices tend to use rapid, jerky movements.

6. If you're using vocal commentary such as "We're in Frontierland now, looking toward Thunder Mountain Railroad," be sure to speak loudly because the background noise of the parks may muffle your words.

7. Don't film into the sun.

8. Camcorder filming is allowed inside attractions, even those that forbid flash photography.

9. Film events such as parades, character shows, and theater-style attractions such as the Country Bear Vacation Hoedown or the Indiana Jones Epic Stunt Spectacular, which are especially fun to watch once you're home.

WHAT'S NEW?

Orlando changes size and shape faster than Alice in Wonderland. My husband and I laugh at the memory of one of our earlier visits, when we got utterly lost on I-4, zooming past exits with him shrieking "I thought you said you knew this town!" while I clutched a 1977 map and muttered "But I swear that lake wasn't here last year."

If you've been away from WDW for 2 years or longer, these attractions will be new to you:

- the entire Disney-MGM Studios Theme Park
- Mickey's Starland in the MK
- Dreamflight in Tomorrowland in the MK
- Norway pavilion at Epcot
- Wonders of Life at Epcot

- Typhoon Lagoon
- Pleasure Island

In addition, the Caribbean Beach and the Grand Floridian resorts and the Walt Disney World Swan and Dolphin are all "new" on-site hotels.

Index

Fast-food restaurants
  in Disney-MGM Studios, 125–126
  in Epcot Center, 108
  in Magic Kingdom, 81–82
Fiesta Fun Center, Contemporary
  Resort, 184
50's Prime Time Cafe, 124
Filming at studios, 128
Fireworks, 142, 155
First aid, 178
Fishing, 146
Five-day touring plan, 51–56
5-day pass, 5, 6
  cost of, 17
Food. *See* Restaurants
Fort Liberty, 156
Fort Wilderness Campground
  Resort, 10, 32–33
4-day pass, 5
  cost of, 17
4-day touring plan, 51–56
Fourth of July, 5
Frontierland
  attractions of, 74–77
  touring tips, 72
Frontierland Shootin' Arcade, 75
Future World
  attractions of, 94–100
  touring plan for, 93

Gatorland Zoo, 149
Geography, 7
Golf, 146–147
  junior golf, 147
Grand Floridian Beach Resort,
  26–27
  Mouseketeer Clubhouses, 158
  Victoria and Albert's, 162
  World Passkey Packages, 13
Grand Floridian Cafe, 178
Grand Prix Raceway, 70
Great Movie Ride, The, 119
  scare factor of, 126–127

Haifeng, 37
  child care at, 159
Hall of Presidents, The, 77–78
Haunted Mansion, The, 78
  scare factor in, 86
Health studies, 6–7
Height requirements for rides, 19
Henson, Jim, 123

Hilton at Disney Village Hotel
  Plaza, 36
  child care at, 158–159
Hollywood & Vine Cafeteria of the
  Stars, 125
Hollywood Brown Derby, 124–125
Hoop-Dee-Doo Musical Revue, 143,
  156–157
  reservations for, 17
Horizons, 97
Horseback riding, 147
Hotels
  choosing of, 23–39
  Epcot Center hotels, 33–34
  future hotels, 38–39
  general information on, 35–36
  information from, 170–171
  Magic Kingdom resorts, 26–33
  off-site hotels, 11–12, 36–38
  on-site hotels, 9–11
  package trips, 12–14
  reservations for, 17
  ticket purchase at, 16–17
  Value Season, 35–36
Hours of operation, 5
Hurricane season, 4
Hyatt Regency Grand Cypress
  Resort, 38

IllumiNations, 109–110, 143,
  154–155
Impressions de France, 101
Indiana Jones Epic Stunt Spectacu-
  lar, 122
Infant services. *See* Baby services
Information services, 170–171
Insulin refrigeration, 170
It's a Small World, 65

Jackson, Michael, 97
Jogging trails, 147
Journey into Imagination, 96–97
  at night, 155
  scare factor, 112–113
Jungle Cruise, 73
  scare factor in, 86

KinderCare, 157–158
Kingdom Suites Hotel, 39
King Henry's Feast, 156
King Stefan's Banquet Hall, 80–81